PREPOSITIONS.

The syntax of Prepositions consists, not solely or mainly in their power of governing the objective case, (though this alone is the scope which most grammarians have given it,) but in their adaptation to the other terms between which they express certain relations, such as appear by the sense of the words uttered.

RULE XXIII.—PREPOSITIONS.

Prepositions show the relations of words, and of the things or thoughts expressed by them: as; "He came *from* Rome *to* Paris, *in* the company *of* many eminent men, and passed *with* them *through* many cities"—*Analectic Magazine.*

> "Ah! who can tell the triumphs *of* the mind, *By* truth illumin'd, and
> *by* taste refin'd?"—*Rogers.*

EXCEPTION FIRST.

The preposition *to*, before an abstract infinitive, and at the head of a phrase which is made the subject of a verb, has no proper antecedent term of relation; as, "*To* learn to die, is the great business of life."—*Dillwyn.* "Nevertheless, *to* abide in the flesh, is more needful for you."—ST. PAUL: *Phil.*, i, 24. "*To* be reduced to poverty, is a great affliction."

"Too much *to* know, is, to know nought but fame;
And every godfather can give a name."—*Shakspeare.*

EXCEPTIONSECOND.

The preposition *for,* when it introduces its object before an infinitive, and the whole phrase is made the subject of a verb, has properly no antecedent term of relation; as, "*For* us to learn to die, is the great business of life."—"Nevertheless, *for* me to abide in the flesh, is more needful for you."—"*For* an old man to be reduced to poverty is a very great affliction."

"*For* man to tell how human life began, Is hard; for who himself beginning knew?"—*Milton.*

OBSERVATIONSONRULEXXIII.

OBS. 1.—In parsing any ordinary preposition, the learner should name the *two terms* of the relation, and apply the foregoing rule, after the manner prescribed in Praxis 12th of this work. The principle is simple and etymological, being implied in the very definition of a preposition, yet not the less necessary to be given as a rule of syntax. Among tolerable writers, the prepositions exhibit more errors than any other equal number of words. This is probably owing to the careless manner in which they are usually slurred over in parsing. But the parsers, in general, have at least this excuse, that their text-books have taught them no better; they therefore call the preposition *a preposition*, and leave its use and meaning unexplained.

OBS. 2.—If the learner be at any loss to discover the true terms of relation, let him ask and answer *two questions*: first, with the interrogative *what* before the preposition, to find the antecedent; and then, with the same pronoun after the preposition, to find the subsequent term. These questions

English Grammar

Parts of Speech, General Review, General Rule, Prepositions, and Interjections

Virginia D. Elser

answered according to the sense, will always give the true terms. For example: "They dashed that rapid torrent through."—*Scott.* Ques. *What* through? Ans. "*Dashed through.*" Ques. Through *what?* Ans. "*Through that torrent.*" For the meaning is—"They dashed through that rapid torrent." If one term is perfectly obvious, (as it almost always is,) find the other in this way; as, "Day unto day uttereth speech, and night unto night showeth knowledge."—*Psal.*, xix, 2. Ques. *What* unto day? Ans. "*Uttereth unto day.*" Ques. *What* unto night? Ans. "*Showeth unto night*" For the meaning is —"Day uttereth speech unto day, and night showeth knowledge unto night." To parse rightly, is, to understand rightly; and what is well expressed, it is a shame to misunderstand or misinterpret. But sometimes the position of the two nouns is such, that it may require some reflection to find either; as,

"Or that choice plant, so grateful to the nose,
Which *in* I know not what far country grows."—*Churchill*, p. 18.

OBS. 3.—When a preposition *begins* or *ends* a sentence or clause, the terms of relation, if both are given, are transposed; as, "To a studious *man,* action is a relief."—*Burgh.* That is, "Action is a relief *to* a studious man." "*Science* they [the ladies] do not *pretend* TO."—*Id.* That is, "They do not pretend *to* science." "Until I have done that *which* I *have spoken* to thee OF."—*Gen.*, xxviii, 15. The word governed by the preposition is always the subsequent term of the relation, however it may be placed; and if this be a relative pronoun, the transposition is permanent. The preposition, however, may be put before any relative, except *that* and *as*; and this is commonly thought to be its most appropriate place: as, "Until I have done that *of which* I have spoken to thee," Of the placing of it last, Lowth says, "This is an idiom *which* our language is strongly inclined *to*;" Murray and others, "This is an idiom *to which* our language is strongly inclined:" while they all add, "it prevails in common conversation, and suits very well with the familiar style in writing; but the placing of the preposition before the relative, is more graceful, as well as more perspicuous, and agrees much better with the solemn and elevated style."—*Lowth's Gram.*, p. 95; *Murray's*, 8vo, p. 200; *Fisk's*, 141; *R. C. Smiths*, 167; *Ingersoll's*, 227; *Churchill's*. 150.

OBS. 4.—The terms of relation between which a preposition may be used, are very various. The *former* or *antecedent* term may be a noun, an adjective, a pronoun, a verb, a participle, or an adverb: and, in some instances, we find not only one preposition put before an other, but even a conjunction or an interjection used on this side; as, "*Because* OF offences."—"*Alas* FOR him!"—The *latter* or *subsequent* term, which is the word governed by the preposition, may be a noun, a pronoun, a pronominal adjective, an infinitive verb, or an imperfect or preperfect participle: and, in some instances, prepositions appear to govern adverbs, or even whole phrases. See the observations in the tenth chapter of Etymology.

OBS. 5.—Both terms of the relation are usually expressed; though either of them may, in some instances, be left out, the other being given: as, (1.) THE FORMER—"All shall know me, [*reckoning*] FROM the least to the greatest."—*Heb.*, viii, 11. [*I say*] "IN a word, it would entirely defeat the purpose."—*Blair*. "When I speak of reputation, I mean not only [*reputation*] IN regard to knowledge, but [*reputation*] IN regard to the talent of communicating knowledge."—*Campbell's Rhet.*, p. 163; *Murray's Gram.*, i, 360. (2.) THE LATTER—"Opinions and ceremonies [*which*] they would die FOR."—*Locke*. "IN [*those*] who obtain defence, or [*in those*] who defend."—*Pope*. "Others are more modest than [*what*] this comes TO."—*Collier's Antoninus*, p. 66.

OBS. 6.—The only proper exceptions to the foregoing rule, are those which are inserted above, unless the abstract infinitive used as a predicate is also to be excepted; as, "In both, to reason right, is *to* submit."—*Pope*. But here most if not all grammarians would say, the verb "*is*" is the antecedent term, or what their syntax takes to govern the infinitive. The relation, however, is not such as when we say, "He *is to submit*;" that is, "He *must submit*, or *ought to submit*;" but, perhaps, to insist on a different mode of parsing the more separable infinitive or its preposition, would be a needless refinement. Yet some regard ought to be paid to the different relations which the infinitive may bear to this finite verb. For want of a due estimate of this difference, the following sentence is, I think, very faulty: "The great business of this life *is to prepare*, and *qualify us*, for the enjoyment of a better."—*Murray's Gram.*, Vol. i, p. 373. If the author meant to tell what our great business in this life is, he should rather have said: "The great business of this life is, to prepare and qualify *ourselves* for the enjoyment of a better."

OBS. 7.—In relation to the infinitive, Dr. Adam remarks, that, "*To* in English is often taken *absolutely*; as, *To* confess the truth; *To* proceed; *To* conclude."—*Latin and Eng. Gram.*, p. 182. But the assertion is not entirely true; nor are his examples appropriate; for what he and many other grammarians call the *infinitive absolute*, evidently depends on something *understood*; and the preposition is, surely, in no instance independent of what follows it, and is therefore never entirely absolute. Prepositions are not to be supposed to have no antecedent term, merely because they stand at the head of a phrase or sentence which is made the subject of a verb; for the phrase or sentence itself often contains that term, as in the following example: "*In* what way mind acts upon matter, is unknown." Here *in* shows the relation between *acts* and *way*; because the expression suggests, that mind *acts* IN *some way* upon matter.

OBS. 8.—The second exception above, wherever it is found applicable, cancels the first; because it introduces an antecedent term before the preposition *to*, as may be seen by the examples given. It is questionable too, whether both of them may not also be cancelled in an other way; that is, by transposition and the introduction of the pronoun *it* for the nominative: as, "*It* is a great *affliction*, TO *be reduced* to poverty."—"*It* is *hard* FOR *man* to tell how human life began."—"Nevertheless *it* is more needful for you, THAT *I should abide* in the flesh." We cannot so well say, "It is more needful *for you*, FOR *me to abide* in the flesh;" but we may say, "It is, *on your account*, more needful FOR *me to abide* in the flesh." If these, and other similar examples, are not to be accounted additional instances in which *to* and *for*, and also the conjunction that, are without any proper antecedent terms, we must suppose these particles to show the relation between what precedes and what follows them.

OBS. 9.—The preposition (as its name implies) *precedes* the word which it governs. Yet there are some exceptions. In the familiar style, a preposition governing a relative or an interrogative pronoun, is often separated from its object, and connected with the other term of relation; as, "*Whom* did he speak *to*?" But it is more dignified, and in general more graceful, to place the preposition before the pronoun; as, "*To whom* did he speak?" The relatives *that* and *as*, if governed by a preposition, must always precede it. In some instances, the pronoun must be supplied in parsing; as, "To set off the banquet [*that* or *which*] he gives notice *of*."—*Philological Museum*, i, 454. Sometimes the objective word is put first because it is emphatical; as, "*This* the great understand, *this* they pique themselves *upon*."—*Art of Thinking*, p. 66. Prepositions of more than one syllable, are sometimes put immediately after their objects, especially in poetry; as, "Known all the *world over*."—*Walker's Particles* p. 291. "The thing is known all *Lesbos over*."—*Ibid*.

"Wild Carron's lonely *woods among*."—*Langhorne*.

"Thy deep *ravines* and *dells along*."—*Sir W. Scott*.

OBS. 10.—Two prepositions sometimes come together; as, "Lambeth is *over against* Westminster abbey."—*Murray's Gram.*, i, 118. "And *from before* the lustre of her face, White break the clouds away."—*Thomson*. "And the meagre fiend Blows mildew *from between* his shrivell'd lips."— *Cowper*. These, in most instances, though they are not usually written as compounds, appear naturally to coalesce in their syntax, as was observed in the tenth chapter of Etymology, and to express a sort of compound relation between the other terms with which they are connected. When such is their character, they ought to be taken together in parsing; for, if we parse them separately, we must either call the first an adverb, or suppose some very awkward ellipsis. Some instances however occur, in which an object may easily be supplied to the former word, and perhaps ought to be; as, "He is at liberty to sell it *at* [a price] *above* a fair remuneration."— *Wayland's Moral Science*, p. 258. "And I wish they had been at the bottom of the ditch I pulled you out of, *instead of* [being] *upon* my back."—*Sandford and Merton*, p. 29. In such examples as the following, the first preposition, *of*, appears to me to govern the plural noun which ends the sentence; and the intermediate ones, *from* and *to*, to have both terms of their relation *understood*: "Iambic verse consists *of from* two *to* six feet; that is, *of from* four *to* twelve syllables."—*Blair's Gram.*, p. 119. "Trochaic verse consists *of from* one to three feet."—*Ibid.* The meaning is—"Iambic verse consists *of feet* varying in number from two to six; or (it consists) *of syllables* varying from four to twelve."—"Trochaic verse consists *of feet* varying from one *foot* to three *feet*."

OBS. 11.—One antecedent term may have several prepositions depending on it, with one object after each, or more than one after any, or only one after both or all; as, "A declaration *for* virtue and *against* vice."— *Butler's Anal.*, p. 157. "A positive law *against* all fraud, falsehood, *and* violence, and *for*, or *in* favour *of*, all justice *and* truth." "For *of* him, and *through* him, and *to* him, are all things."—*Bible*. In fact, not only may the relation be simple in regard to all or any of the words, but it may also be complex in regard to all or any of them. Hence several different prepositions, whether they have different antecedent terms or only one and the same, may refer either jointly or severally to one object or to more. This follows, because not only may either antecedents or objects be connected by conjunctions, but prepositions also admit of this construction, with or without a connecting of their antecedents. Examples: "They are capable *of*, and placed *in*, different stations in the society of mankind."—*Butler's Anal.*, p. 115. "Our perception *of* vice *and* ill desert arises *from*, and is the result *of*, a comparison *of* actions *with* the nature *and* capacities *of* the agent."—*Ib.*, p. 279. "And the design *of* this chapter is, *to* inquire how far this is the case; how far, *over and above* the moral nature which God has given us, *and* our natural notion *of* him, as righteous governor *of* those his creatures *to* whom he has given this nature; I say, how far, *besides* this, the principles *and* beginnings *of* a moral government *over* the world may be discerned, *notwithstanding and amidst* all the confusion *and* disorder *of* it."—*Ib.*, p. 85.

OBS. 12.—The preposition *into*, expresses a relation produced by motion or change; and *in*, the same relation, without reference to motion as having produced it: hence, "to walk *into* the garden," and, "to walk *in* the garden," are very different in meaning. "It is disagreeable to find a word split *into* two by a pause."—*Kames, El. of Crit.*, ii, 83. This appears to be right in sense, but because brevity is desirable in unemphatic particles, I suppose most persons would say, "split *in* two." In the Bible we have the phrases, "rent *in* twain,"—"cut *in* pieces,"—"brake *in* pieces the rocks,"—"brake all their bones *in* *pieces*,"—"brake them *to* pieces,"—"broken *to* pieces,"—"pulled *in* pieces." In all these, except the first, *to* may perhaps be considered preferable to *in*; and *into* would be objectionable only because it is longer and less simple. "Half of them dare not shake the snow from off their cassocks, lest they shake themselves *to* pieces."—SHAK.: *Kames*, ii, 246.

OBS. 13.—*Between*, or *betwixt*, is used in reference to two things or parties; *among*, or *amongst, amid*, or *amidst*, in reference to a greater number, or to something by which an other may be surrounded: as, "Thou pendulum *betwixt* a smile and tear."—*Byron*. "The host *between the* mountain and the shore."—*Id*. "To meditate *amongst* decay, and stand a ruin *amidst* ruins."—*Id*. In the following examples, the import of these prepositions is not very accurately regarded; "The Greeks wrote in capitals, and left no spaces between their words."—*Wilson's Essay*, p. 6. This construction may perhaps be allowed, because the spaces by which words are now divided, occur severally *between* one word and an other; but the author might as well have said, "and left no spaces *to distinguish* their words." "There was a hunting match agreed upon *betwixt* a lion, an ass, and a fox."—*L'Estrange*. Here *by* or *among* would, I think, be better than *betwixt*, because the partners were more than two. "*Between* two *or more* authors, different readers will differ, exceedingly, as to the preference in point of merit."—*Campbell's Rhet*., p. 162; *Jamieson's*, 40; *Murray's Gram*., i, 360. Say, "*Concerning* two or more authors," because *between* is not consistent with the word *more*. "Rising *one among another* in the greatest confusion and disorder."—*Spect*., No. 476. Say, "Rising *promiscuously*," or, "Rising *all at once*;" for *among* is not consistent with the distributive term *one an other*.

OBS. 14.—Of two prepositions coming together between the same terms of relation, and sometimes connected in the same construction, I have given several plain examples in this chapter, and in the tenth chapter of Etymology, a very great number, all from sources sufficiently respectable. But, in many of our English grammars, there is a stereotyped remark on this point, originally written by Priestley, which it is proper here to cite, as an other specimen of the Doctor's hastiness, and of the blind confidence of certain compilers and copyists: "Two different prepositions *must be improper* in the same construction, and in the same sentence: [as,] *The combat* between *thirty Britons,* against *twenty English.* Smollett's Voltaire, Vol. 2, p. 292."—*Priestley's Gram.,* p. 156. Lindley Murray and others have the same remark, with the example altered thus: "The combat *between* thirty *French against* twenty English."—*Murray's Gram.,* 8vo, p. 200; *Smith's New Gram.,* 167: *Fisk's,* 142; *Ingersoll's,* 228. W. Allen has it thus: "Two different prepositions in the *same construction* are improper; as, a combat *between twenty* French *against thirty* English."—*Elements of E. Gram.,* p. 179. He gives the odds to the latter party. Hiley, with no expense of thought, first takes from Murray, as he from Priestley, the useless remark, "Different relations, and different senses, must be expressed by different prepositions;" and then adds, "*One relation* must not, *therefore,* be expressed by two different prepositions in the same clause; thus, 'The combat *between thirty* French *against thirty* English,' should be, 'The combat *between thirty* French *and thirty* English.'"—*Hiley's E. Gram.,* p 97. It is manifest that the error of this example is not in the use of *two prepositions,* nor is there any truth or fitness in the note or notes made on it by all these critics; for had they said, "The combat *of* thirty French *against* twenty English," there would still be two prepositions, but where would be the impropriety, or where the sameness of construction, which they speak of? *Between* is incompatible with *against,* only because it requires two parties or things for its own regimen; as, "The combat *between* thirty *Frenchmen and* twenty *Englishmen.*" This is what Smollett should have written, to make sense with the word "*between.*"

OBS. 15.—With like implicitness, Hiley excepted, these grammarians and others have adopted from Lowth an observation in which the learned doctor has censured quite too strongly the joint reference of different prepositions to the same objective noun: to wit, "Some writers separate the preposition from its noun, in order to connect different prepositions to the same noun; as, 'To suppose the zodiac and planets to be efficient *of*, and antecedent *to*, themselves.' Bentley, Serm. 6. This [construction], whether in the familiar or the solemn style, is *always inelegant*; and *should never be admitted*, but in forms of law, and the like; where fullness and exactness of expression must take *place* of every other consideration."—*Lowth's Gram.*, p. 96; *Murray's*, i, 200; *Smith's*, 167; *Fisk's*, 141; *Ingersoll's*, 228; *Alger's*, 67; *Picket's*, 207. Churchill even goes further, both strengthening the censure, and disallowing the exception: thus, "This, whether in the solemn or in the familiar style, is *always* inelegant, and should *never be admitted*. It is an *awkward shift* for avoiding the repetition of a word, *which might be accomplished without it* by any person who has the least command of language."—*New Gram.*, p. 341. Yet, with all their command of language, not one of these gentlemen has told us how the foregoing sentence from Bentley may be *amended*; while many of their number not only venture to use different prepositions before the same noun, but even to add a phrase which puts that noun in the nominative case: as, "Thus, the time of the infinitive may be *before, after*, or *the same as*, the time of the governing verb, according as the *thing* signified by the infinitive is supposed to be *before, after*, or *present with*, the *thing* denoted by the governing verb."—*Murray's Gram.*, i, 191; *Ingersoll's*, 260; *R. C. Smith's*, 159.

OBS. 16.—The structure of this example not only contradicts palpably, and twice over, the doctrine cited above, but one may say of the former part of it, as Lowth, Murray, and others do, (in no very accurate English,) of the text 1 Cor., ii, 9: "There seems to be an impropriety in this sentence, in which the same noun serves in a double capacity, performing at the same time the *offices both of the nominative and objective cases*."—*Murray's Gram.*, 8vo, p. 224. See also *Lowth's Gram.*, p. 73; *Ingersoll's*, 277; *Fisk's*, 149; *Smith's*, 185. Two other examples, exactly like that which is so pointedly censured above, are placed by Murray under his thirteenth rule for the comma; and these likewise, with all faithfulness, are copied by Ingersoll, Smith, Alger, Kirkham, Comly, Russell, and I know not how many more. In short, not only does this rule of their punctuation include the construction in question; but the following exception to it, which is remarkable for its various faults, or thorough faultiness, is applicable to *no other*: "Sometimes, when the *word* with which the *last* preposition *agrees*, is *single*, it is better to *omit* the comma before it: as, 'Many states were in alliance *with*, and under the protection *of* Rome.'"—*Murray's Gram.*, p. 272; *Smith's*, 190; *Ingersoll's*, 284; *Kirkham's*, 215; *Alger's*, 79; *Alden's*, 149; *Abel Flint's*, 103; *Russell's*, 115. But the blunders and contradictions on this point, end not here. Dr. Blair happened most unlearnedly to say, "What is called splitting of particles, or separating a preposition from the noun which it governs, is *always to be avoided*. As if I should say, 'Though virtue borrows no assistance from, yet it may often be accompanied by, the advantages of fortune.'"—*Lect. XII*, p. 112. This too, though the author himself did not *always* respect the rule, has been thought worthy to be copied, or stolen, with all its faults! See *Jamieson's Rhetoric*, p. 93; and *Murray's Octavo Gram.*, p. 319.

OBS. 17.—Dr. Lowth says, "The noun *aversion*, (that is, a turning away,) as likewise the adjective *averse*, seems to require the preposition *from* after it; and not so properly to admit of *to*, or *for*, which are often used with it."—*Gram.*, p. 98. But this doctrine has not been adopted by the later grammarians: "The words *averse* and *aversion* (says Dr. Campbell) are more properly construed with *to* than with *from*. The examples in favour of the latter preposition, are beyond comparison outnumbered by those in favour of the former."—*Murray's Gram.*, i, 201; *Fisk's*, 142; *Ingersoll's*, 229. This however must be understood only of mental aversion. The expression of Milton, "On the coast *averse from* entrance," would not be improved, if *from* were changed to *to*. So the noun *exception*, and the verb to *except*, are sometimes followed by *from*, which has regard to the Latin particle *ex,* with which the word commences; but the noun at least is much more frequently, and perhaps more properly, followed by *to.* Examples: "Objects of horror must be *excepted from* the foregoing theory."—*Kames, El. of Crit.,* ii, 268. "*From* which there are but two *exceptions,* both of them rare."—*Ib.,* ii. 89. "*To* the rule that fixes the pause after the fifth portion, there is one *exception,* and no more."—*Ib.,* ii, 84. "No *exception* can be taken *to* the justness of the figure."—*Ib.,* ii, 37. "Originally there was no *exception* from the rule."—*Lowth's Gram.,* p. 58. "*From* this rule there is mostly an *exception.*"—*Murray's Gram.,* i, 269. "But *to* this rule there are many *exceptions.*"—*Ib.,* i. 240. "They are not to be regarded as exceptions *from* the rule,"—*Campbell's Rhet.,* p. 363.

OBS. 18.—After correcting the example. "He *knows* nothing *on* [of] it," Churchill remarks, "There seems to be a strange perverseness among the *London vulgar* in perpetually substituting *on* for *of,* and *of* for *on.*"—*New Gram.,* p. 345. And among the expressions which Campbell censures under the name of *vulgarism,* are the following: "'Tis my humble request you will be particular in speaking *to* the following points."—*Guardian,* No. 57. "The preposition ought to have been *on.* Precisely of the same stamp is the *on't* for *of it,* so much used by one class of writers."—*Philosophy of Rhet.,* p. 217. So far as I have observed, the use of *of* for *on* has never been frequent; and that of *on* for *of,* or *on't* for *of it,* though it may never have been a polite custom, is now a manifest *archaism,* or imitation of ancient usage. "And so my young Master, whatever comes *on't,* must have a Wife look'd out for him."—*Locke, on Ed.,* p. 378. In Saxon, *on* was put for more than half a dozen of our present prepositions. The difference between *of* and *on* or *upon,* appears in general to be obvious enough; and yet there are some phrases in which it is not easy to determine which of these words ought to be preferred: as, "Many things they cannot *lay hold on* at once."—HOOKER: *Joh. Dict.* "Uzzah put forth his hand to the ark of God, and *took hold of* it."—2 SAM.: *ib.* "Rather thou shouldst *lay hold upon* him."—BEN

JONSON: *ib.* "Let them find courage to *lay hold on* the occasion."—MILTON: *ib.* "The hand is fitted to *lay hold of* objects."—RAY: *ib.* "My soul *took hold on* thee."—ADDISON: *ib.* "To *lay hold of* this safe, this only method of cure."—ATTERBURY: *ib.* "And *give* fortune no more *hold* of him."—DRYDEN: *ib.* "And his laws *take* the surest *hold of* us."—TILLOTSON: *ib.* "It will then be impossible you can *have* any *hold upon* him."—SWIFT: *ib.* "The court of Rome gladly *laid hold on* all the opportunities."—*Murray's Key,* ii, p. 198. "Then did the officer *lay hold of* him and execute him."—*Ib.,* ii, 219. "When one can *lay hold upon* some noted fact."—*Blair's Rhet.,* p. 311. "But when we would *lay* firm *hold of* them."—*Ib.,* p. 28. "An advantage which every one is glad to *lay hold of.*"—*Ib.,* p. 75. "To have *laid* fast *hold of* it in his mind."—*Ib.,* p. 94. "I would advise them to lay aside their common-places, and to *think* closely *of* their subject."—*Ib.,* p. 317. "Did they not *take hold of* your fathers?"—*Zech.,* i, 6. "Ten men shall *take hold of* the skirt of one that is a Jew."—*Ib.,* viii, 23. "It is wrong to say, either 'to *lay* hold *of* a thing,' or 'to *take* hold *on* it.'"—*Blair's Gram.,* p. 101. In the following couplet, *on* seems to have been preferred only for a rhyme:

"Yet, lo! in me what authors have to *brag on*!
Reduc'd at last to hiss in my own dragon."—*Pope.*

OBS. 19.—In the allowable uses of prepositions, there may perhaps be some room for choice; so that what to the mind of a critic may not appear the fittest word, may yet be judged not positively ungrammatical. In this light I incline to view the following examples: "Homer's plan is still more defective, *upon* another account."—*Kames, El. of Crit.,* ii, 299. Say—"*on an other* account." "It was almost eight *of the* clock before I could leave that variety of objects."—*Spectator,* No. 454. Present usage requires—"eight *o*'clock." "The Greek and Latin writers had a considerable advantage *above* us."—*Blair's Rhet.,* p. 114. "The study of oratory has this advantage *above* that of poetry."—*Ib.*, p. 338. "A metaphor has frequently an advantage *above* a formal comparison."— *Jamieson's Rhet.*, p. 150. This use of *above* seems to be a sort of Scotticism: an Englishman, I think, would say —"advantage *over* us," &c. "Hundreds have all these crowding upon them from morning *to* night."— *Abbott's Teacher*, p. 33. Better—"from morning *till* night." But Horne Tooke observes, "We apply TO indifferently to *place* or *time*; but TILL to *time* only, and never to *place*. Thus we may say, 'From morn TO night th' eternal larum rang;' or, 'From morn TILL night.' &c."— *Diversions of Purley*, i, 284.

NOTEST ORULEXXIII.

NOTE I.—Prepositions must be chosen and employed agreeably to the usage and idiom of the language, so as rightly to express the relations intended. Example of error: "By which we arrive *to* the last division."— *Richard W. Green's Gram.*, p. vii. Say,—"arrive *at*." NOTE II.—Those prepositions which are particularly adapted in meaning to *two objects*, or to *more*, ought to be confined strictly to the government of such terms only as suit them. Example of error: "What is *Person*? It is the *medium of* distinction *between* the *speaker*, the *object* addressed or spoken *to*, and the *object* spoken *of*."—*O. B. Peirce's Gram.*, p. 34. "*Between three*" is an incongruity; and the text here cited is bad in several other respects.

NOTE III.—An *ellipsis* or *omission* of the preposition is inelegant, except where long and general use has sanctioned it, and made the relation sufficiently intelligible. In the following sentence, *of* is needed: "I will not flatter you, that all I see in you is *worthy love*."— *Shakspeare*. The following requires *from*: "Ridicule *is banished France*, and is losing ground in England."—*Kames, El. of Crit.*, i, 106.

NOTE IV.—The *insertion* of a preposition is also inelegant, when the particle is needless, or when it only robs a transitive verb of its proper regimen; as, "The people of England may congratulate *to* themselves."—DRYDEN: *Priestley's Gram.*, p. 163. "His servants ye are, *to* whom ye obey."—*Rom.*, vi, 16.

NOTE V.—The preposition and its object should have that position in respect to other words, which will render the sentence the most perspicuous and agreeable. Examples of error: "Gratitude is a forcible and active principle in good and generous minds."—*Murray's Key*, 8vo, p. 169. Better: "In good and generous minds, gratitude is a forcible and active principle." "By a single stroke, he knows how to reach the heart."— *Blair's Rhet.*, p. 439. Better: "He knows how to reach the heart by a single stroke."

IMPROPRIETIESFORCORRECTION.

FALSESYNT AXUNDERRULEXXIII.

EXAMPLESUNDERNOTEI.—CHOICEOFPREPOSITIONS.

"You have bestowed your favours to the most deserving persons."— *Swift, on*
E. Tongue.

[FORMULE.—Not proper because the relation between *have bestowed* and *persons* is not correctly expressed by the preposition *to*. But, according to Note 1st under Rule 23d, "Prepositions must be chosen and employed agreeably to the usage and idiom of the language, so as rightly to express the relations intended." This relation would be better expressed by *upon*; thus, "You have bestowed your favours *upon* the most deserving persons."]

"But to rise beyond that, and overtop the crowd, is given to few."—*Blair's Rhet.*, p. 351. "This also is a good sentence, and gives occasion to no material remark."—*Ib.*, p. 201. "Though Cicero endeavours to give some reputation of the elder Cato, and those who were his cotemporaries."—*Ib.*, p. 245. "The change that was produced on eloquence, is beautifully described in the Dialogue."—*Ib.*, p. 249. "Without carefully attending to the variation which they make upon the idea."—*Ib.*, p. 367. "All of a sudden, you are transported into a lofty palace."—*Hazlitt's Lect.*, p. 70. "Alike independent on one another."—*Campbell's Rhet.*, p. 398. "You will not think of them as distinct processes going on independently on each other,"—*Channing's Self-Culture*, p. 15. "Though we say, to *depend on*, *dependent on*, and *independent on*, we say, *independently of*."—*Churchill's Gram.*, p. 348. "Independently on the rest of the sentence."—*Lowth's Gram.*, p. 78; *Guy's*, 88; *Murray's*, i, 145 and 184; *Ingersoll's*, 150; *Frost's*, 46; *Fisk's*, 125; *Smith's New Gram.*, 156; *Gould's Lat. Gram.*, 209; *Nixon's Parser*, 65. "Because they stand independent on the rest of the sentence."—*Fisk's Gram.*, p. 111. "When a substantive is joined with a participle in English independently in the rest of the sentence."—*Adam's Lat. and Eng. Gram., Boston Ed. of 1803*, p. 213; *Albany Ed. of 1820*, p. 166. "Conjunction, comes of the two Latin words *con*, together, and *jungo*, to join."—*Merchant's School Gram.*, p. 19. "How different to this is the life of Fulvia!"—*Addison's Spect.*, No. 15. "*Loved* is a participle or adjective, derived of the word *love*."—*Dr. Ash's Gram.*, p. 27. "But I would inquire at him, what an office is?"—*Barclay's Works*, iii, 463. "For the capacity is brought unto action."—*Ib.*, iii, 420. "In this period, language and taste arrive to purity."—*Webster's Essays*, p. 94. "And should you not aspire at distinction in the republick of letters."—*Kirkham's Gram.*, p. 13. "Delivering you up to the synagogues, and in prisons."—*Keith's Evidences*, p. 55. "One that is kept from falling in a ditch, is as truly saved, as he that is taken out of one."—*Barclay's Works*, i, 312. "The best on it is, they are but a sort of French Hugonots."—*Addison, Spect.*, No. 62. "These last Ten Examples are indeed of a different Nature to the former."—*Johnson's Gram. Com.*, p. 333. "For the initiation of students in the principles of the English language."—ANNUAL REVIEW: *Murray's Gram.*, ii, 299. "Richelieu profited of every circumstance which the conjuncture afforded,"—*Bolingbroke, on Hist.*, p. 177. "In the names of drugs and plants, the mistake in a word may endanger life."—*Murray's Key*, ii, 165. "In order to the carrying on its several parts into execution."—*Butler's Analogy*, p. 192. "His abhorrence to the superstitious figure."—HUME: *Priestley's Gram.*, p. 164. "Thy prejudice to my cause."—DRYDEN: *ib.*, p. 164. "Which is found among every species of liberty."—HUME: *ib.*, p. 169. "In a hilly region to the north of Jericho."—*Milman's Jews*, Vol. i, p. 8. "Two or more singular nouns, coupled with AND, require a verb and pronoun in the plural."—*Lennie's Gram.*, p. 83.

"Books should to one of these four ends conduce,
For wisdom, piety, delight, or use."—*Denham*, p. 239.

UNDERNOTE II.—TWO OBJECTS OR MORE.

"The Anglo-Saxons, however, soon quarrelled between themselves for precedence."—*Constable's Miscellany*, xx, p. 59. "The distinctions between the principal parts of speech are founded in nature."—*Webster's Essays*, p. 7. "I think I now understand the difference between the active, passive, and neuter verbs."—*Ingersoll's Gram.*, p. 124. "Thus a figure including a space between three lines, is the real as well as nominal essence of a triangle."—*Locke's Essay*, p. 303. "We must distinguish between an imperfect phrase, a simple sentence, and a compound sentence."—*Lowth's Gram.*, p. 117; *Murray's*, i, 267; *Ingersoll's*, 280; *Guy's*, 97. "The Jews are strictly forbidden by their law, to exercise usury among one another."—*Sale's*

Koran, p. 177. "All the writers have distinguished themselves among one another."—*Addison.* "This expression also better secures the systematic uniformity between the three cases."—*Nutting's Gram.*, p. 98. "When a disjunctive occurs between two or more Infinitive Modes, or clauses, the verb must be singular."— *Jaudon's Gram.*, p. 95. "Several nouns or pronouns together in the same case, not united by *and*, require a comma between each."—*Blair's Gram.*, p. 115. "The difference between the several vowels is produced by opening the mouth differently, and placing the tongue in a different manner for each."—*Churchill's Gram.*, p. 2. "Thus feet composed of syllables, being pronounced with a sensible interval between each, make a more lively impression than can be made by a continued sound."—*Kames, El. of Crit.*, Vol. ii, p. 32. "The superlative degree implies a comparison between three or more."—*Smith's Productive Gram.*, p. 51. "They are used to mark a distinction between several objects."—*Levizac's Gram.*, p. 85.

UNDERNOTEIII.—OMISSIONOFPREPOSITIONS.

"This would have been less worthy notice."—*Churchill's Gram.*, p. 197. "But I passed it, as a thing unworthy my notice."—*Werter.* "Which, in compliment to me, perhaps, you may, one day, think worthy your attention."—*Bucke's Gram.*, p. 81. "To think this small present worthy an introduction to the young ladies of your very elegant establishment."— *Ib.*, p. iv. "There are but a few miles portage."—*Jefferson's Notes on Virginia*, p. 17. "It is worthy notice, that our mountains are not solitary."—*Ib.*, p. 26. "It is of about one hundred feet diameter."— *Ib.*, 33. "Entering a hill a quarter or half a mile."—*Ib.*, p. 47. "And herself seems passing to that awful dissolution, whose issue is not given human foresight to scan."—*Ib.*, p. 100. "It was of a spheroidical form, of about forty feet diameter at the base, and had been of about twelve feet altitude."—*Ib.*, p. 143. "Before this it was covered with trees of twelve inches diameter, and round the base was an excavation of five feet depth and width."—*Ibid.* "Then thou mayest eat grapes thy fill at thine own pleasure."—*Deut.*, xxiii, 24. "Then he brought me back the way of the gate of the outward sanctuary."—*Ezekiel*, xliv, 1. "They will bless God that he has peopled one half the world with a race of freemen."—*Webster's Essays*, p. 94. "What use can these words be, till their meaning is known?"—*Town's Analysis*, p. 7. "The tents of the Arabs now are black, or a very dark colour."—*The Friend*, Vol. v, p. 265. "They may not be unworthy the attention of young men."—*Kirkham's Elocution*, p. 157. "The pronoun that is frequently applied to persons, as well as things."— *Merchant's Gram.*, p. 87. "And *who* is in the same case that *man* is."—*Sanborn's Gram.*, p. 148. "He saw a flaming stone, apparently about four feet diameter."—*The Friend*, vii, 409. "Pliny informs us, that this stone was the size of a cart."—*Ibid.* "Seneca was about twenty years of age in the fifth year of Tiberius, when the Jews were expelled Rome."—*Seneca's Morals*, p. 11. "I was prevented[438] reading a letter which would have undeceived me."—*Hawkesworth, Adv.*, No. 54. "If the problem can be solved, we may be pardoned the inaccuracy of its demonstration."—*Booth's Introd.*, p. 25. "The army must of necessity be the school, not of honour, but effeminacy."—*Brown's Estimate*, i. 65. "Afraid of the virtue of a nation, in its opposing bad measures."—*Ib.*, i, 73. "The uniting them in various ways, so as to form words, would be easy."—*Music of Nature*, p. 34. "I might be excused taking any more notice of it."—*Watson's Apology*, p. 65. "Watch therefore; for ye know not what hour your Lord doth come."—*Matt.*, xxiv, 42. "Here, not even infants were spared the sword."—*M'Ilvaine's Lectures*, p. 313. "To prevent men turning aside to corrupt modes of worship."—*Calvin's Institutes*, B. I, Ch. 12, Sec. 1. "God expelled them the Garden of Eden."—*Burder's Hist.*, Vol. i, p. 10. "Nor could he refrain expressing to the senate the agonies of his mind"—*Art of Thinking*, p. 123. "Who now so strenuously opposes the granting him any new powers."—*Duncan's Cicero*,

p. 127. "That the laws of the censors have banished him the forum."—*Ib.*, p. 140. "We read not that he was degraded his office any other way."—*Barclay's Works*, iii, 149. "To all whom these presents shall come, Greeting."—*Hutchinson's Mass.*, i, 459. "On the 1st, August, 1834."—*British Act for the Abolition of Slavery.*

> "Whether you had not some time in your life
> Err'd in this point which now you censure him."—*Shak.*

UNDERNOTEIV .—OFNEEDLESSPREPOSITIONS.

"And the apostles and elders came together to consider of this matter."—*Barclay's Works*, i, 481. "And the apostles and elders came together for to consider of this matter."—*Acts*, xv, 6. "Adjectives in our Language have neither Case, Gender, nor Number; the only Variation they have is by Comparison."—*Buchanan's Gram.*, p. 27. "'It is to you, that I am indebted for this privilege;' that is, 'to you am I indebted;' or, 'It is to you to whom I am indebted.'"—*Sanborn's Gram.*, p. 232. "*Books* is a noun, of the third person, plural number, of neuter gender,"— *Ingersoll's Gram.*, p. 15. "*Brother's* is a common substantive, of the masculine gender, the third person, the singular number, and in the possessive case."—*Murray's Gram.*, i, 229. "*Virtue's* is a common substantive, of the third person, the singular number, and in the possessive case."—*Ib.*, i, 228. "When the authorities on one side greatly preponderate, it is in vain to oppose the prevailing usage."—*Campbell's Rhet.*, p. 173; *Murray's Gram.*, i, 367. "A captain of a troop of banditti, had a mind to be plundering of Rome."—*Collier's Antoninus*, p. 51. "And, notwithstanding of its Verbal power, we have added the *to* and other signs of exertion."—*Booth's Introd.*, p. 28. "Some of these situations are termed CASES, and are expressed by additions to the Noun instead of by separate words."—*Ib.*, p. 33. "Is it such a fast that I have chosen, that a man should afflict his soul for a day, and to bow down his head like a bulrush?"—*Bacon's Wisdom*, p. 65. "And this first emotion comes at last to be awakened by the accidental, instead of, by the necessary antecedent."—*Wayland's Moral Science*, p. 17. "At about the same time, the subjugation of the Moors was completed."—*Balbi's Geog.*, p. 269. "God divided between the light and between the darkness."— *Burder's Hist.*, i, 1. "Notwithstanding of this, we are not against outward significations of honour."—*Barclay's Works*, i, 242. "Whether these words and practices of Job's friends, be for to be our rule."—*Ib.*, i, 243. "Such verb cannot admit of an objective case after it."—*Lowth's Gram.*, "For which God is now visibly punishing of these Nations."—*Right of Tythes*, "In this respect, Tasso yields to no poet, except to Homer."—*Blair's Rhet.*, "Notwithstanding of the numerous panegyrics on the ancient English liberty."—HUME: *Priestley's Gram.*, "Their efforts seemed to anticipate on the spirit, which became so general afterwards."—*Id., ib.*, p. 167.

UNDERNOTEV .—THEPLACINGOFTHEWORDS.

"But how short are my expressions of its excellency!"—*Baxter*. "There is a remarkable union in his style, of harmony with ease."—*Blair's Rhet.*, "It disposes in the most artificial manner, of the light and shade, for viewing every thing to the best advantage."—"Aristotle too holds an eminent rank among didactic writers for his brevity."—"In an introduction, correctness should be carefully studied in the expression."—"Precision is to be studied, above all things in laying down a method."—"Which shall make the impression on the mind of something that is one, whole and entire."—"At the same time, there are some defects which must be acknowledged in the Odyssey."—"Beauties, however, there are, in the concluding books, of the tragic kind."—"These forms of conversation by degrees multiplied and grew troublesome."—*Spectator*, No. 119. "When she has made her own choice, for form's sake, she sends a congé-d'-élire to her friends."—"Let us endeavour to establish to ourselves an interest in him who holds the reins of the whole creation in his hand."—"Let us endeavour to establish to ourselves an interest in him, who, in his hand, holds the reins of the whole creation."—*Kames, El. of Crit.*, ii, 53. "The most frequent measure next to this in English poetry is that of eight syllables."—*Blair's Gram.*, "To introduce as great a variety as possible of cadences."—*Jamieson's Rhet.*, "He addressed several exhortations to them suitable to their circumstances."—*Murray's Key*, ii, "Habits must be acquired of temperance and self-denial."—"In reducing the rules prescribed to practice."—*Murray's Gram.*, "But these parts must be so closely bound together as to make the impression upon the mind, of one object, not of many."—*Blair's Rhet.*, "Errors are sometimes committed by the most distinguished writer, with respect to the use of *shall* and *will*"—*Butler's Pract. Gram.*,

INTERJECTIONS.

Interjections, being seldom any thing more than natural sounds or short words uttered independently, can hardly be said to have any *syntax*; but since some rule is necessary to show the learner how to dispose of them in parsing, a brief axiom for that purpose, is here added, which completes our series of rules: and, after several remarks on this canon, and on the common treatment of Interjections, this chapter is made to embrace *Exercises* upon all the other parts of speech, that the chapters in the Key may correspond to those of the Grammar.

RULE XXIV.—INTERJECTIONS.

Interjections have no dependent construction; they are put absolute, either alone, or with other words: as, "*O!* let not thy heart despise me."—*Dr. Johnson.* "*O* cruel *thou*!"—*Pope, Odys.*, B. xii, l. 333. "Ah wretched *we*, poets of earth!"—*Cowley*,

> "*Ah Dennis! Gildon ah!* what ill-starr'd rage
> Divides a friendship long confirm'd by age?"
> *Pope, Dunciad*, B. iii,

OBSERVATIONS ON RULE XXIV.

OBS. 1.—To this rule, there are properly *no exceptions*. Though interjections are sometimes uttered in close connexion with other words, yet, being mere signs of passion or of feeling, they seem not to have any strict grammatical relation, or dependence according to the sense. Being destitute alike of relation, agreement, and government, they must be used independently, if used at all. Yet an emotion signified in this manner, not being causeless, may be accompanied by some object, expressed either by a nominative absolute, or by an adjective after *for*: as, "*Alas!* poor *Yorick!*"— *Shak.* Here the grief denoted by *alas*, is certainly *for Yorick*; as much so, as if the expression were, "Alas *for* poor Yorick!" But, in either case, *alas*, I think, has no dependent construction; neither has *Yorick,* in the former, unless we suppose an ellipsis of some governing word.

OBS. 2.—The interjection *O* is common to many languages, and is frequently uttered, in token of earnestness, before nouns or pronouns put absolute by direct address; as, "Arise, *O Lord; O God,* lift up thine hand."— *Psalms,* x, 12. "*O ye* of little faith!"—*Matt.,* vi, 30. The Latin and Greek grammarians, therefore, made this interjection the *sign* of the *vocative case*; which case is the same as the nominative put absolute by address in English. But this particle is no positive index of the vocative; because an independent address may be made without that sign, and the *O* may be used where there is no address: as, "*O* scandalous want! *O* shameful omission!"—"Pray, *Sir,* don't be uneasy."—*Burgh's Speaker*, p. 86.

OBS. 3.—Some grammarians ascribe to two or three of our interjections the power of governing sometimes the nominative case, and sometimes the objective. First, NIXON; in an exercise entitled, "NOMINATIVE GOVERNED BY AN INTERJECTION," thus: "The interjections O! Oh! and Ah! *require* after them the nominative case of a *substantive* in the *second* person; as, 'O thou *persecutor!*'—'O Alexander! thou hast slain thy friend.' *O* is an interjection, *governing* the nominative case *Alexander.*"—

English Parser, Again, under the title, "OBJECTIVE CASE GOVERNED BY AN INTERJECTION," he says: "The interjections O! Oh! and Ah! *require* after them the objective case of a *substantive* in the *first* or *third* person; as, 'Oh *me!*' 'Oh the *humiliations*!' *Oh* is an interjection, *governing* the objective case *humiliations*."—These two rules are in fact contradictory, while each of them absurdly suggests that *O, oh,* and *ah,* are used only with nouns. So J. M. PUTNAM: "Interjections sometimes *govern* an objective case; as, *Ah me! O* the tender *ties! O* the soft *enmity! O me* miserable! *O* wretched *prince! O* cruel *reverse* of fortune! When an address is made, the interjection does not perform the office of government."—*Putnam's Gram.,* So KIRKHAM; who, under a rule quite different from these, extends the doctrine of government to *all* interjections: "According to the genius of the English language, transitive verbs and prepositions *require* the objective case of a noun or pronoun after them; and this requisition is all that is meant by *government,* when we say that these parts of speech *govern the objective* case. THE SAME PRINCIPLE APPLIES TO THE INTERJECTION. 'Interjections *require* the objective case of a pronoun of the first person after them; but the nominative of a noun or pronoun of the second or third person; as, Ah *me!* Oh *thou!* O my *country!*' To say, then, that interjections *require* particular cases after them, is synonymous with saying, that they *govern* those cases; and this office of the interjection is in *perfect accordance* with that which it performs in the Latin, and many other languages."—*Kirkham's Gram.,* According to this, every interjection has as much need of an object after it, as has a transitive verb or a preposition! The rule has, certainly, *no* "accordance" with what occurs in Latin, or in any other language; it is wholly a fabrication, though found, in some shape or other, in well-nigh all English grammars.

OBS. 4.—L. MURRAY'S doctrine on this point is thus expressed: "The interjections *O! Oh!* and *Ah! require* the objective case of a pronoun in the first person after them, as, 'O me! oh me! Ah me!' But the nominative case in the second person: as, 'O thou persecutor!' 'Oh ye hypocrites!' 'O thou, who dwellest,' &c."—*Octavo Gram.*, INGERSOLL copies this most faulty note literally, adding these words to its abrupt end,—i. e., to its inexplicable "&c." used by Murray; "because the first person *is governed by a preposition* understood: as, 'Ah *for* me!' or, 'O what will become of me!' &c., and the second person is in the *nominative independent*, there being a direct address."—*Conversations on E. Gram.*, So we see that this grammarian and Kirkham, both modifiers of Murray, understand their master's false verb "*require*" very differently. LENNIE too, in renouncing a part of Murray's double or threefold error, "*Oh! happy us!*" for, "*O* happy *we!*" teaches thus: "Interjections sometimes *require* the objective case after them, but they never *govern* it. In the first edition of this grammar," says he, "I followed Mr. Murray and others, in leaving *we*, in the exercises to be turned into *us*; but that it should be *we*, and not *us*, is obvious; because it is the nominative to *are* understood; thus, *Oh* happy *are we*, or, *Oh we are* happy, (being) surrounded with so many blessings."—*Lennie's Gram., Fifth Edition, Twelfth*, Here is an other solution of the construction of this pronoun of the first person, contradictory alike to Ingersoll's, to Kirkham's, and to Murray's; while *all are wrong*, and this among the rest. The word should indeed be *we*, and not *us*; because we have both analogy and good authority for the former case, and nothing but the false conceit of sundry grammatists for the latter. But it is a *nominative absolute*, like any other nominative which we use in the same exclamatory manner. For the first person may just as well be put in the nominative absolute, by exclamation, as any other; as, "Behold *I* and the *children* whom God hath given me!"—*Heb.*, "Ecce *ego* et *pueri* quos mihi dedit Deus!"—*Beza*. "O brave *we!*"—*Dr. Johnson, often*. So Horace: "O *ego* lævus," &c.—*Ep. ad Pi.*, 301.

"Ah! luckless *I!* who purge in spring my spleen—
Else sure the first of bards had Horace been."
—*Francis's Hor.*, ii, 209.

OBS. 5.—Whether Murray's remark above, on "*O! Oh! and Ah!*" was originally designed for a *rule of government* or not, it is hardly worth any one's while to inquire. It is too lame and inaccurate every way, to deserve any notice, but that which should serve to explode it forever. Yet no few, who have since made English grammars, have copied the text literally; as they have, for the public benefit, stolen a thousand other errors from the same quarter. The reader will find it, with little or no change, in Smith's New Grammar, p. 96 and 134; Alger's, 56; Allen's, 117; Russell's, 92; Blair's, 100, Guy's, 89; Abel Flint's, 59; A Teacher's, 43, Picket's, 210; Cooper's[439] Murray, 136; Wilcox's, 95; Bucke's, 87; Emmons's, 77; and probably in others. Lennie varies it *indefinitely*, thus: "RULE. The interjections *Oh!* and *Ah!* &c. *generally* require the objective case of the first personal pronoun, *and* the nominative of the second; as, Ah *me!* O *thou* fool! O *ye* hypocrites!"—*Lennie's Gram.*, p. 110; *Brace's*, 88. M'Culloch, after Crombie, thus: "RULE XX. Interjections are joined with the objective case of the pronoun of the first person, and with the nominative of the pronoun of the second; as, Ah me! O ye hypocrites."—*Manual of E. Gram.*, p. 145; and *Crombie's Treatise*, p. 315; also *Fowler's E. Language*, p. 563. Hiley makes it a note, thus: "The interjections. O! Oh! Ah! *are followed by* the objective case of a pronoun of the first person; as, *'Oh me!' 'Ah me!'* but by the nominative case of the pronoun in the second person; as, *'O thou* who dwellest.' "—*Hiley's Gram.*, p. 82. This is what the same author elsewhere calls "THE GOVERNMENT OF INTERJECTIONS;" though, like some others, he had set it in the "Syntax of PRONOUNS." See *Ib.*, p. 108. Murray, in forming his own little "Abridgment," omitted it altogether. In his other grammars, it is still a mere note, standing where he at first absurdly put it, under his rule for the agreement of pronouns with their antecedents. By many of his sage amenders, it has been placed in the catalogue of principal rules. But, that it is no adequate rule for interjections, is manifest; for, in its usual form, it is limited to *three*, and none of these can ever, with any propriety, be parsed by it. Murray himself has not used it in any of his forms of parsing. He conceived, (as I hinted before in Chapter 1st,) that, "The syntax of the Interjection is of *so very limited a nature,* that it *does not require* a distinct, appropriate rule."—*Octavo Gram.,* i. 224.

OBS. 6.—Against this remark of Murray's, a good argument may be drawn from the ridiculous use which has been made of his own suggestion in the other place. For, though that suggestion never had in it the least shadow of truth, and was never at all applicable either to the three interjections, or to pronouns, or to cases, or to the persons, or to any thing else of which it speaks, it has not only been often copied literally, and called a "RULE" of syntax, but many have, yet more absurdly, made it a *general canon* which imposes on all interjections a syntax that belongs to none of them. For example: "*An interjection must be followed* by the objective case of a pronoun in the first person; *and* by a nominative of the second person; as—*Oh me! ah me! oh thou! AH hail, ye* happy men!"—*Jaudon's Gram.,* p. 116. This is as much as to say, that every interjection must have a pronoun or two after it! Again: "*Interjections must be followed* by the objective case of the pronoun in the first person; as, O *me!* Ah *me!* and by the nominative case of the second person; as, O *thou* persecutor! Oh *ye* hypocrites!"—*Merchant's Murray,* p. 80; *Merchant's School Gram.,* p. 99. I imagine there is a difference between O and *oh,*[440] and that this author, as well as Murray, in the first and the last of these examples, has misapplied them both. Again: "*Interjections require* the objective case of a pronoun of the first person, and the nominative case of the second; as, *Ah me! O thou*"—*Frost's El. of E. Gram.,* p. 48. This, too, is general, but equivocal; as if one case or both were necessary to each interjection!

OBS. 7.—Of *nouns,* or of the *third person,* the three rules last cited say nothing;[441] though it appears from other evidence, that their authors supposed them applicable at least to *some nouns* of the *second person.* The supposition however was quite needless, because each of their grammars contains an other Rule, that, "When an address is made, the noun or pronoun is in the nominative case *independent*;" which, by the by, is far from being universally true, either of the noun or of the pronoun. Russell imagines, "The words *depending* upon interjections, have so near a resemblance to those in a direct address, that they may very properly be classed under the same general head," and be parsed as being, "in the nominative case *independent*." See his "*Abridgment of Murray's Grammar*," p. 91. He does not perceive that *depending* and *independent* are words that contradict each other. Into the same inconsistency, do nearly all those gentlemen fall, who ascribe to interjections a control over cases. Even Kirkham, who so earnestly contends that what any words *require* after them they must necessarily *govern*, forgets his whole argument, or justly disbelieves it, whenever he parses any noun that is uttered with an interjection. In short, he applies his principle to nothing but the word *me* in the phrases, "*Ah me!*" "*Oh me!*" and "*Me miserable!*" and even these he parses falsely. The second person used in the vocative, or the nominative put absolute by direct address, whether an interjection be used or not, he rightly explains as being "in the nominative case independent;" as, "O *Jerusalem, Jerusalem!*"—*Kirkham's Gram.*, p. 130. "O *maid* of Inistore!"— *Ib.*, p. 131. But he is wrong in saying that, "Whenever a noun is of the second person, it is in the nominative case independent;" (*Ib.*, p. 130;) and still more so, in supposing that, "The principle contained in the note" [which tells what interjections *require*,] "*proves* that every noun of the second person is in the nominative case."—*Ib.*, p. 164. A falsehood proves nothing but the ignorance or the wickedness of him who utters it. He is wrong too, as well as many others, in supposing that this nominative independent is not a nominative absolute; for, "The vocative is [*generally*, if not *always*,] absolute."—*W. Allen's Gram.*, p. 142. But that nouns of the second person are not always absolute or independent, nor always in the nominative case, or the vocative, appears, I think, by the following example: "This is the stone which was set at nought *of you builders*."— *Acts,* iv, II. See Obs. 3d on Rule 8th.

OBS. 8.—The third person, when uttered in exclamation, with an interjection before it, is parsed by Kirkham, not as being governed by the interjection, either in the nominative case, according to his own argument and own rule above cited, or in the objective, according to Nixon's notion of the construction; nor yet as being put absolute in the nominative, as I believe it generally, if not always is; but as being "the nominative to a verb understood; as, 'Lo,' *there is* 'the poor *Indian*!' '0, the *pain*' *there is!* 'the *bliss*' *there is* 'IN dying!'"—*Kirkham's Gram.*, p. 129. Pope's text is, "*Oh* the pain, the bliss *of* dying!" and, in all that is here changed, the grammarian has perverted it, if not in all that he has added. It is an other principle of Kirkham's Grammar, though a false one, that, "Nouns have but two persons, the second and [the] third."—P. 37. So that, these two being disposed of agreeably to his own methods above, which appear to include the second and third persons of pronouns also, there remains to him nothing but the objective of the pronoun of the first person to which he can suppose his other rule to apply; and I have shown that there is no truth in it, even in regard to this. Yet, with the strongest professions of adhering to the principles, and even to "the language" of Lindley Murray, this gentleman, by copying somebody else in preference to "that eminent philologist," has made himself one of those by whom Murray's erroneous remark on *O, oh,* and *ah,* with pronouns of the first and second persons, is not only stretched into a rule for all interjections, but made to include nouns of the second person, and both nouns and pronouns of the third person: as, "Interjections require the objective case of a pronoun of the first person after them, but the nominative of a noun or pronoun of the second or third person; as, 'Ah! *me*; Oh! *thou*; O! *virtue*!'"—*Kirkham's Gram.*, 2d Ed., p. 134; Stereotype Ed., p. 177. See the same rule, with examples and punctuation different, in his

Stereotype Edition, p. 164; *Comly's Gram.*, 116; *Greenleaf's*, 36; and *Fisk's*, 144. All these authors, except Comly, who comes much nearest to the thing, profess to present to us "*Murray's Grammar Simplified*;" and this is a sample of their work of *simplification*!—an ignorant piling of errors on errors!

"O imitatores servum pecus! ut mihi sæpe
Bilem, sæpe jocum vestri movêre tumultus!"—*Horace.*

OBS. 9.—Since so many of our grammarians conceive that interjections require or govern cases, it may be proper to cite some who teach otherwise. "Interjections, in English, have no government."—*Lowth's Gram.*, p. 111. "Interjections have no government, or admit of no construction."—*Coar's Gram.*, p. 189. "Interjections have no connexion with other word's."—*Fuller's Gram.*, p. 71. "The interjection, in a grammatical sense, is totally unconnected with every other word in a sentence. Its arrangement, of course, is altogether arbitrary, and cannot admit of any theory."—*Jamieson's Rhet.*, p. 83. "Interjections cannot properly have either concord or government. They are only mere sounds excited by passion, and have no just connexion with any other part of a sentence. Whatever case, therefore, is joined with them, must depend on some other word understood, except the vocative, which is always placed absolutely."—*Adam's Latin Gram.*, p. 196; *Gould's*, 193. If this is true of the Latin language, a slight variation will make it as true of ours. "Interjections, and phrases resembling them, are taken absolutely; as, *Oh*, world, *thy slippery turns*! But the phrases Oh *me*! and Ah *me*! frequently occur."—*W. Allen's Gram.*, p. 188. This passage is, in several respects, wrong; yet the leading idea is true. The author entitles it, "SYNTAX OF INTERJECTIONS," yet absurdly includes in it I know not what *phrases*! In the phrase, "*thy slippery turns!*" no word is absolute, or "taken absolutely" but this noun "*turns*;" and this, without the least hint of its *case*, the learned author will have us to understand to be absolute, because the phrase *resembles an interjection!* But the noun "*world*" which is also absolute, and which still more resembles an interjection, he will have to be so for a different reason—because it is in what he chooses to call the *vocative case.* But, according to custom, he should rather have put his interjection absolute *with* the noun, and written it, "*O world*," and not, "*Oh, world.*" What he meant to do with "*Oh me!* and *Ah me!*" is doubtful. If any phrases come fairly under his rule, these are the very ones; and yet he seems to introduce them as exceptions! Of these, it can hardly be said, that they "*frequently* occur." Lowth notices only the latter, which he supposes elliptical. The former I do not remember to have met with more than three or four times; except in grammars, which in this case are hardly to be called authorities: "*Oh! me*, how fared it with me then?"—*Job Scott.* "*Oh me!* all the horse have got over the river, what shall we do?"—WALTON: *Joh. Dict.*

"But when he was first seen, *oh me!*
What shrieking and what misery!"—*Wordsworth's Works*, p. 114.

OBS. 10.—When a declinable word not in the nominative absolute, follows an interjection, as part of an imperfect exclamation, its construction (if the phrase be good English) depends on something understood; as, "Ah *me!*"—that is, "Ah! *pity* me;" or, "Ah! *it grieves* me;" or, as some will have it, (because the expression in Latin is "*Hei mihi!*") "Ah *for* me!"—*Ingersoll.* "Ah! *wo is to* me."—*Lowth.* "Ah! *sorrow is to* me."—*Coar.* So of "*oh me!*" for, in these expressions, if not generally, *oh* and *ah* are exactly equivalent the one to the other. As for "*O me*" it is now seldom met with, though Shakspeare has it a few times. From these examples, O. B. Peirce erroneously imagines the "independent case" of the pronoun *I* to be *me*, and accordingly parses the word without supposing an ellipsis; but in the plural he makes that case to be *we*, and not *us*. So, having found an example of "Ah *Him!*" which, according to one half of our grammarians, is bad

English, he conceives the independent case of *he* to be *him*; but in the plural, and in both numbers of the words *thou* and *she*, he makes it the nominative, or the same in form as the nominative. So builds he "the temple of Grammatical consistency!"—P. 7. Nixon and Cooper must of course approve of "*Ah him!*" because they assume that the interjection *ah* "*requires*" or "*governs*" the objective case of the third person. Others must condemn the expression, because they teach that *ah* requires the nominative case of this person. Thus Greenleaf sets down for false syntax, "O! happy *them*, surrounded with so many blessings!"—*Gram. Simplified*, p. 47. Here, undoubtedly, the word should be *they*; and, by analogy, (if indeed the instances are analogous,) it would seem more proper to say, "Ah *he!*" the nominative being our only case absolute. But if any will insist that "*Ah him!*" is good English, they must suppose that *him* is governed by something understood; as, "Ah! I *lament* him;" or, "Ah! *I mourn for* him." And possibly, on this principle, the example referred to may be most correct as it stands, with the pronoun in the objective case: "*Ah Him!* the first great martyr in this great cause."—D. WEBSTER: *Peirce's Gram.*, p. 199.

OBS. 11.—If we turn to the Latin syntax, to determine by analogy what case is used, or ought to be used, after our English interjections, in stead of finding a "perfect accordance" between that syntax and the rule for which such accordance has been claimed, we see at once an utter repugnance, and that the pretence of their agreement is only a sample of Kirkham's unconscionable pedantry. The rule, in all its modifications, is based on the principle, that the choice of *cases* depends on the distinction of *persons*—a principle plainly contrary to the usage of the Latin classics, and altogether untrue. In Latin, some interjections are construed with the nominative, the accusative, or the vocative; some, only with the dative; some, only with the vocative. But, in English, these four cases are all included in two, the nominative and the objective; and, the case independent or absolute being necessarily the nominative, it follows that the objective, if it occur after an interjection, must be the object of something which is capable of governing it. If any disputant, by supposing ellipses, will make objectives of what I call nominatives absolute, so be it; but I insist that interjections, in fact, never "require" or "govern" one case more than an other. So Peirce, and Kirkham, and Ingersoll, with pointed self-contradiction, may continue to make "the independent case," whether vocative or merely exclamatory, the subject of a verb, expressed or understood; but I will content myself with endeavouring to establish a syntax not liable to this sort of objection. In doing this, it is proper to look at all the facts which go to show what is right, or wrong. "*Lo, the poor Indian!*" is in Latin, "*Ecce pauper Indus!*" or, "*Ecce pauperem Indum!*" This use of either the nominative or the accusative after *ecce*, if it proves any thing concerning the case of the word *Indian*, proves it doubtful. Some, it seems, pronounce it an objective. Some, like Murray, say nothing about it. Following the analogy of our own language, I refer it to the nominative absolute, because there is nothing to determine it to be otherwise. In the examples. "*Heu me miserum!* Ah *wretch* that I am!"—(*Grant's Latin Gram.*, p. 263.) and "*Miser ego homo!* O wretched *man* that I am!"—(*Rom.*, vii, 24,) if the word *that* is a relative pronoun, as I incline to think it is, the case of the nouns *wretch* and *man* does not depend on any other words, either expressed or implied. They are therefore nominatives absolute, according to Rule 8th, though the Latin words may be most properly explained on the principle of ellipsis.

OBS. 12.—Of some impenetrable blockhead, Horace, telling how himself was vexed, says: "*O te*, Bollane, cerebri Felicem! aiebam tacitus."—*Lib.* i, *Sat.* ix, 11. Literally: "*O thee*, Bollanus, happy of brain! said I to myself." That is, "O! *I envy* thee," &c. This shows that *O* does not "require the nominative case of the second person" after it, at least, in Latin. Neither does *oh* or *ah*: for, if a governing word be suggested, the objective may be proper; as, "Whom did he injure? Ah! *thee*, my boy?"—or even the possessive; as, "Whose sobs do I hear? Oh! *thine*, my child?" Kirkham tells us truly, (Gram., p. 126,) that the exclamation "*O my*" is frequently heard in conversation. These last resemble Lucan's use of the genitive, with an ellipsis of the governing noun: "*O miseræ sortis!*" i.e., "*O* [men] *of miserable lot!*" In short, all the Latin cases as well as all the English, may possibly occur after one or other of the interjections. I have instanced all but the ablative, and the following is literally an example of that, though the word *quanto* is construed adverbially: "Ah, *quanto* satius est!"—*Ter. And.,* ii, 1. "Ah, *how much* better it is!" I have also shown, by good authorities, that the nominative of the first person, both in English and in Latin, may be properly used after those interjections which have been supposed to require or govern the objective. But how far is analogy alone a justification? Is "*O thee*" good English, because "*O te*" is good Latin? No: nor is it bad for the reason which our grammarians assign, but because our best writers never use it, and because *O* is more properly the sign of the vocative. The literal version above should therefore be changed; as, "O Bollanus, *thou* happy numskull! said I to myself."

OBS. 13—Allen Fisk, "author of Adam's Latin Grammar Simplified," and of "Murray's English Grammar Simplified," sets down for "*False Syntax*" not only that hackneyed example, "Oh! happy we," &c., but, "O! You, who love iniquity," and, "Ah! you, who hate the light."—*Fisk's E. Gram.*, p. 144. But, to imagine that either *you* or *we* is wrong here, is certainly no sing of a great linguist; and his punctuation is very inconsistent both with his own rule of syntax and with common practice. An interjection set off by a comma or an exclamation point, is of course put absolute *singly*, or by itself. If it is to be read as being put absolute with something else, the separation is improper. One might just as well divide a preposition from its object, as an interjection from the case which it is supposed to govern. Yet we find here not only such a division as Murray sometimes improperly adopted, but in one instance a total separation, with a capital following; as, "O! You, who love iniquity," for, "O you who love iniquity!" or "O ye," &c. If a point be here set between the two pronouns, the speaker accuses all his hearers of loving iniquity; if this point be removed, he addresses only such as do love it. But an interjection and a pronoun, each put absolute singly, one after the other, seem to me not to constitute a very natural exclamation. The last example above should therefore be, "Ah! you hate the light." The first should be written, "*O* happy we!"

OBS. 14.—In other grammars, too, there are many instances of some of the errors here pointed out. R. C. Smith knows no difference between *O* and *oh*; takes "*Oh!* happy *us*" to be accurate English; sees no impropriety in separating interjections from the pronouns which he supposes them to "govern;" writes the same examples variously, even on the same page; inserts or omits commas or exclamation points at random; yet makes the latter the means by which interjections are to be known! See his *New Gram.*, pp. 40, 96 and 134. Kirkham, who lays claim to "a new system of punctuation," and also stoutly asserts the governing power of interjections, writes, and rewrites, and finally stereotypes, in one part of his book. "Ah me! *Oh* thou! O my country!" and in an other, "Ah! me; *Oh!* thou; O! virtue." See Obs. 3d and Obs. 8th above. From such hands, any thing "*new*" should be received with caution: this last specimen of his scholarship has more errors than words.

OBS. 15.—Some few of our interjections seem to admit of a connexion with other words by means of a preposition or the conjunction *that* as, "O *to* forget her!"—*Young.* "O *for* that warning voice!"—*Milton.* "O *that* they were wise!"—*Deut.,* xxxii, 29. "O *that* my people had hearkened unto me!"—*Ps.,* lxxxi, 13, "Alas *for* Sicily!"—*Cowper.* "O *for* a world in principle as chaste As this is gross and selfish!"—*Id.* "Hurrah *for* Jackson!"—*Newspaper.* "A bawd, sir, fy *upon* him!"—SHAK.: *Joh. Dict.* "And fy *on* fortune, mine avowed foe!"—SPENCER: *ib.* This connexion, however, even if we parse all the words just as they stand, does not give to the interjection itself any dependent construction. It appears indeed to refute Jamieson's assertion, that, "The interjection is *totally unconnected* with every other word in a sentence;" but I did not quote this passage, with any averment of its accuracy; and, certainly, many nouns which are put absolute themselves, have in like manner a connexion with words that are not put absolute: as, "O *Lord* God of hosts, hear my prayer; give ear, O *God* of Jacob. Selah."—*Ps.,* lxxxiv, 8. But if any will suppose, that in the foregoing examples something else than the interjection must be the antecedent term to the preposition or the conjunction, they may consider the expressions elliptical: though it must be confessed, that much of their vivacity will be lost, when the supposed ellipses are supplied: as, "O! *I desire* to forget her."—"O! *how I long* for that warning voice!"—"O! *how I wish* that they were wise!"—"Alas! I *wail* for Sicily."—"Hurrah! *I shout* for Jackson."—"Fy! *cry out* upon him." Lindley Murray has one example of this kind, and if his punctuation of it is not bad in all his editions, there must be an ellipsis in the expression: "O! *for* better times."—*Octavo Gram.,* ii, 6;

Duodecimo Exercises, p. 10. He also writes it thus: "O. *for* better times."—*Octavo Gram.*, i, 120; *Ingersoll's Gram.*, p. 47. According to common usage, it should be, "O for better times!"

OBS. 16.—The interjection may be placed at the *beginning* or the *end* of a simple sentence, and sometimes *between* its less intimate parts; but this part of speech is seldom, if ever, allowed to interrupt the connexion of any words which are closely united in sense. Murray's definition of an interjection, as I have elsewhere shown, is faulty, and directly contradicted by his example: "O virtue! how amiable thou art!"—*Octavo Gram.*, i, 28 and 128; ii. 2. This was a favourite sentence with Murray, and he appears to have written it uniformly in this fashion; which, undoubtedly, is altogether right, except that the word *"virtue"* should have had a capital Vee, because the quality is here personified.

OBS. 17.—Misled by the false notion, that the term *interjection* is appropriate only to what is "thrown in between the parts of a *sentence*," and perceiving that this is in fact but rarely the situation of this part of speech, a recent critic, (to whom I should owe some acknowledgements, if he were not wrong in every thing in which he charges me with error,) not only denounces this name as "*barbarous*," preferring Webster's loose term, "*exclamation*;" but avers, that, "The words called *interjection* should *never* be so used—should *always stand alone*; as, 'Oh! virtue, how amiable thou art.' 'Oh? Absalom, my son.' G. Brown," continues he, "drags one into the middle of a sentence, *where it never belonged*; thus, 'This enterprise, *alas*! will never compensate us for the trouble and expense with which it has been attended.' If G. B. meant the *enterprize* of studying grammar, in the old theories, his sentiment is very appropriate; but his *alas*! he should have known enough to have put into the right place:—before the sentence representing the fact that excites the emotion expressed by *alas*! See on the Chart part 3, of RULE XVII. An *exclamation* must *always precede* the phrase or sentence describing the fact that excites the emotion to be expressed by the *exclamation*; as: Alas! I have alienated my friend! *Oh! Glorious hope of bliss secure!*"—*Oliver B. Peirce's Gram.*, p. 375. "O Glorious hope of bliss secure!"—*Ib.*, p. 184. "O *glorious* hope!"—*Ib.*, p. 304.

OBS. 18.—I see no reason to believe, that the class of words which have always, and almost universally, been called *interjections*, can ever be more conveniently explained under any other name; and, as for the term *exclamation*, which is preferred also by Cutler, Felton, Spencer, and S. W. Clark, it appears to me much less suitable than the old one, because it is less specific. Any words uttered loudly in the same breath, are *an exclamation*. This name therefore is too general; it includes other parts of speech than interjections; and it was but a foolish whim in Dr. Webster, to prefer it in his dictionaries. When David "cried *with a loud voice*, O my son Absalom! O Absalom, my son, my son!" [442] he uttered *two* exclamations, but they included all his words. He did not, like my critic above, set off his first word with an interrogation point, or any other point. But, says Peirce, "These words are *used in exclaiming, and are what all know them to be, exclamations*; as I call them. May I not *call* them what they *are*?"—*Ibid.* Yes, truly. But to *exclaim* is to *cry out*, and consequently every *outcry* is an *exclamation*; though there are two chances to one, that *no interjection* at all be used by the bawler. As good an argument, or better, may be framed against every one of this gentleman's professed improvements in grammar; and as for his punctuation and orthography, any reader may be presumed capable of seeing that they are not fit to be proposed as models.

OBS. 19.—I like my position of the word "*alas*" better than that which Peirce supposes to be its only right place; and, certainly, his rule for the location of words of this sort, as well as his notion that they must stand alone, is as false, as it is new. The obvious misstatement of Lowth, Adam,

Gould, Murray, Churchill, Alger, Smith, Guy, Ingersoll, and others, that, "Interjections are words thrown in between the parts of *a sentence*," I had not only excluded from my grammars, but expressly censured in them. It was not, therefore, to prop any error of the old theorists, that I happened to set one interjection "*where*" according to this new oracle, "*it never belonged*." And if any body but he has been practically misled by their mistake, it is not I, but more probably some of the following authors, here cited for his refutation: "I fear, *alas!* for my life."—*Fisk's Gram.*, p. 89. "I have been occupied, *alas!* with trifles."—*Murray's Gr., Ex. for Parsing*, p. 5; *Guy's*, p. 56. "We eagerly pursue pleasure, but, *alas!* we often mistake the road."—*Smith's New Gram.*, p. 40, "To-morrow, *alas!* thou *mayest* be comfortless!"—*Wright's Gram.*, p. 35. "Time flies, *O!* how swiftly."—*Murray's Gram.*, i, 226. "My friend, *alas!* is dead."—*J. Flint's Gram.*, p. 21. "But *John, alas! he* is very idle."—*Merchant's Gram.*, p. 22. "For pale and wan he was, *alas* the while!"—SPENSER: *Joh. Dict.* "But yet, *alas! O* but yet, *alas!* our haps be but hard haps."—SYDNEY: *ib.* "Nay, (what's incredible,) *alack!* I *hardly* hear a woman's clack."—SWIFT: *ib.* "Thus life is spent (*oh fie* upon't!) In being touch'd, and crying—Don't!"—*Cowper*, i, 231. "For whom, *alas!* dost thou prepare The sweets that I was wont to share"—*Id.*, i, 203. "But here, *alas!* the difference lies."—*Id.*, i. 100. "Their names, *alas!* in vain reproach an age," &c.—*Id.*, i, 88. "What nature, *alas!* has denied," &c.—*Id.*, i, 235. "A. *Hail* Sternhold, then; and Hopkins, *hail!* B. Amen."—*Id.*, i 25.

"These Fate reserv'd to grace thy reign divine,
Foreseen by me, but *ah!* withheld from mine!"—*Pope, Dun.*, iii, 215.

IMPROPRIETIES FOR CORRECTION.

FALSE SYNTAX PROMISCUOUS. [Fist] [The following examples of bad grammar, being similar in their character to others already exhibited, are to be corrected, by the pupil, according to formules previously given.]

LESSON I.—ANY PARTS OF SPEECH.

"Such an one I believe yours will be proved to be."—PEET: *Farnum's Gram.*, p. 1. "Of the distinction between the imperfect and the perfect tenses, it may be observed," &c.—*Ainsworth's Gram.*, p. 122. "The subject is certainly worthy consideration."—*Ib.*, p. 117. "By this means all ambiguity and controversy is avoided on this point."—*Bullions, Principles of Eng. Gram., 5th Ed., Pref.*, p. vi. "The perfect participle in English has both an active and passive signification."—*Ib.*, p. 58. "The old house is at length fallen down."—*Ib.*, p. 78. "The king, with the lords and commons, constitute the English form of government."—*Ib.*, p. 93. "The verb in the singular agrees with the person next it."—*Ib.*, p. 95. "Jane found Seth's gloves in James' hat."—*Felton's Gram.*, p. 15. "Charles' task is too great."—*Ibid.*, 15. "The conjugation of a verb is the naming, in regular order, its several modes tenses, numbers and persons."—*Ib.*, p. 24. "The long remembered beggar was his guest."—*Ib.*, 1st Ed., p. 65. "Participles refer to nouns and pronouns."—*Ib.*, p. 81. "F has an uniform sound in every position except in *of*."—*Hallock's Gram.*, 1st Ed., p. 15. "There are three genders; the masculine, the feminine and neuter."—*Ib.*, p. 43. "When *so that* occur together, sometimes the particle *so* is taken as an adverb."—*Ib.*, p. 124. "The definition of the articles show that they modify the words to which they belong."—*Ib.*, p. 138. "The auxiliaries *shall, will*, or *should* is implied."—*Ib.*, p. 192. "Single rhyme trochaic omits the final short syllable."—*Ib.*, p. 244. "Agreeable to this, we read of names being blotted out of God's book,"—BURDER: *ib.*, p. 156; *Webster's Philos. Gram.*, 155; *Improved Gram.*, 107. "The first person is the person speaking."—

Goldsbury's Common School Gram., p. 10. "Accent is the laying a peculiar stress of the voice on a certain letter or syllable in a word."—*Ib.*, Ed. of 1842, p. 75. "Thomas' horse was caught."—*Felton's Gram.*, p. 64. "You was loved."—*Ib.*, p. 45. "The nominative and objective end the same."—*Rev. T. Smith's Gram.*, p. 18. "The number of pronouns, like those of substantives, are two, the singular and the plural."—*Ib.*, p. 22. "*I* is called the pronoun of the *first* person, which is the person speaking."—*Frost's Practical Gram.*, p. 32. "The essential elements of the phrase is an intransitive gerundive and an adjective."—*Hazen's Practical Gram.*, p. 141. "Being rich is no justification for such impudence."—*Ib.*, p. 141. "His having been a soldier in the revolution is not doubted."—*Ib.*, p. 143. "Catching fish is the chief employment of the inhabitants. The chief employment of the inhabitants is catching fish."—*Ib.*, p. 144. "The cold weather did not prevent the work's being finished at the time specified."—*Ib.*, p. 145. "The former viciousness of that man caused his being suspected of this crime."—*Ib.*, p. 145. "But person and number applied to verbs means, certain terminations."—*Barrett's Gram.*, p. 69. "Robert fell a tree."—*Ib.*, p. 64. "Charles raised up."—*Ib.*, p. 64. "It might not be an useless waste of time."—*Ib.*, p. 42. "Neither will you have that *implicit faith* in the writings and works of others which characterise the vulgar,"—*Ib.*, p. 5. "*I*, is the first person, because it denotes the speaker."—*Ib.*, p. 46. "I would refer the student to Hedges' or Watts' Logic."—*Ib.*, p. 15. "Hedge's, Watt's, Kirwin's, and Collard's Logic."—*Parker and Fox's Gram.*, Part III, p. 116. "Letters are called vowels which make a full and perfect sound of themselves."—*Cutler's Gram.*, p. 10. "It has both a singular and plural construction."—*Ib.*, p. 23. "For he beholdest thy beams no more."—*Ib.*, p. 136. "To this sentiment the Committee has the candour to incline, as it will appear by their summing up."—*Macpherson's Ossian, Prelim. Disc.*, p. xviii. "This is reducing the point at issue to a narrow compass."—*Ib.*, p. xxv. "Since the English sat foot upon the soil."—*Exiles of Nova Scotia*, p. 12. "The arrangement of its different parts are easily retained by the memory."—*Hiley's Gram.*, 3d Ed., p. 262. "The words employed are the most appropriate which could have been selected."—*Ib.*, p. 182. "To prevent it launching!"—*Ib.*, p. 135. "Webster has been followed in preference to others, where it differs from them."—*Frazee's Gram.*, p. 8. "Exclamation and Interrogation are often mistaken for one another."—*Buchanan's E. Syntax*, p. 160. "When all nature is hushed in sleep, and neither love nor guilt keep their vigils."—*Felton's Gram.*, p. 96.

"When all nature's hushed asleep,
Nor love, nor guilt, their vigils keep."—*Ib.*, p. 95.

LESSON II.—ANY PARTS OF SPEECH.

"A VERSIFYER and POET are two different Things."—*Brightland's Gram.*, p. 163. "Those Qualities will arise from the well expressing of the Subject."—*Ib.*, p. 165. "Therefore the explanation of *network*, is taken no notice of here."—*Mason's Supplement*, p. vii. "When emphasis or pathos are necessary to be expressed."—*Humphrey's Punctuation*, p. 38. "Whether this mode of punctuation is correct, and whether it be proper to close the sentence with the mark of admiration, may be made a question."—*Ib.*, p. 39. "But not every writer in those days were thus correct."—*Ib.*, p. 59. "The sounds of A, in English orthoepy, are no less than four."—*Ib.*, p. 69. "Our present code of rules are thought to be generally correct."— *Ib.*, p. 70. "To prevent its running into another."—*Humphrey's Prosody*, p. 7. "Shakespeare, perhaps, the greatest poetical genius which England has produced."—*Ib.*, p. 93. "This I will illustrate by example; but prior to which a few preliminary remarks may be necessary."—*Ib.*, p. 107. "All such are entitled to two accents each, and some of which to two accents nearly equal."—*Ib.*, p. 109. "But some cases of the kind are so plain that no one need to exercise his judgment therein."—*Ib.*, p. 122. "I have forbore to use the word."—*Ib.*, p. 127. "The propositions, 'He may study,' 'He might study,' 'He could study,' affirms an ability or power to study."—*Hallock's Gram. of 1842*, p. 76. "The divisions of the tenses has occasioned grammarians much trouble and perplexity."—*Ib.*, p. 77. "By adopting a familiar, inductive method of presenting this subject, it may be rendered highly attractive to young learners."—*Wells's Sch. Gram.*, 1st Ed., p. 1; 3d, 9; 113th, 11. "The definitions and rules of different grammarians were carefully compared with each other."—*Ib.*, *Preface*, p. iii. "So as not wholly to prevent some sounds issuing."—*Sheridan's Elements of English*, p. 64. "Letters of the Alphabet not yet taken notice of."—*Ib.*, p. 11. "IT *is sad*, IT *is strange*, &c., seems to express only that *the thing* is sad, strange, &c."—*The Well-Wishers' Gram.*, p. 68. "THE WINNING is easier than THE PRESERVING a conquest."—*Ib.*, p. 65. "The United States finds itself the owner of a vast region of country at the West."—*Horace Mann in Congress*, 1848. "One or more letters placed before a word is a Prefix."—*S. W. Clark's Pract. Gram.*, p. 42. "One or more letters added to a word is a Suffix."—*Ib.*, p. 42. "Two-thirds of my hair has fallen off."—*Ib.*, p. 126. "'Suspecting,' describes 'we,' by expressing, incidentally, an act of 'we.'"—*Ib.*, p. 130. "Daniel's predictions are now being fulfilled."—*Ib.*, p. 136. "His being a scholar, entitles him to respect."—*Ib.*, p. 141. "I doubted his having been a soldier."—*Ib.*, p. 142. "Taking a madman's sword to prevent his doing mischief, cannot be regarded as robbing him."—*Ib.*, p. 129. "I thought it to be him; but it was not him."—*Ib.*, p. 149. "It was not me that you saw."—*Ib.*, p. 149. "Not to know what happened before you was born, is always to be a boy."—*Ib.*, p. 149. "How long was you going? Three days."—*Ib.*, 158. "The qualifying Adjective is placed next the Noun."—*Ib.*, p. 165. "All went but me."—*Ib.*, p. 93. "This is parsing their own language, and not the author's."—*Wells's School Gram.*, 1st Ed., p. 73. "Nouns which denote males, are of the masculine gender."—*Ib.*, p. 49. "Nouns which denote females, are of the feminine gender."—*Ib.*, p. 49. "When a comparison is expressed between more than two objects of the same class, the superlative degree is employed."—*Ib.*, p. 133. "Where *d* or *t* go before, the additional letter *d* or *t*, in this contracted form, coalesce into one letter with the radical *d* or *t*."—*Dr. Johnson's Gram.*, p. 9. "Write words which will show what kind of a house you live in—what kind of a book you hold in your hand—what kind of a day it is."—*Weld's Gram.*, p. 7. "One word or more is often joined to nouns or pronouns to modify their meaning."—*Ib., 2d Ed.*, p. 30. "*Good* is an adjective; it explains the quality or character of every person or thing to which it is applied."—*Ib.*, p. 33; *Abridg.*, 32. "A great public as well as private advantage arises from every one's devoting himself to that occupation which he prefers, and for which he is specially fitted."—WAYLAND: *Wells's Gram.*, p. 121; *Weld's*, 180. "There was a chance of his recovering his senses. Not thus: 'There was a chance of him recovering his senses.' MACAULEY."—See *Wells's Gram.*, 1st Ed., p. 121; 113th, 135. "This may be known by its not having any connecting word immediately preceding it."—*Weld's Gram., 2d Edition*, p. 181. "There are *irregular* expressions occasionally to be met with, which usage or custom rather than analogy, sanction."—*Ib.*, p. 143. "He added an anecdote of Quinn's relieving Thomson from prison."—*Ib.*, p. 150. "The daily labor of her hands procure for her all that is necessary."—*Ib.*, p. 182. "Its being *me*, need make no change in your determination."—*Hart's Gram.*, p. 128. "The classification of words into what is called the Parts of Speech."—*Weld's Gram.*, p. 5. "Such licenses may be explained under what is usually termed Figures."—*Ib.*, p. 212.

"Liberal, not lavish, is kind nature's hands."—*Ib.*, p. 196.

"They fall successive and successive live."—*Ib.*, p. 213.

LESSON III.—ANY PARTS OF SPEECH.

"A figure of Etymology is the intentional deviation in the usual form of a word."—*Weld's Gram., 2d Edition*, p. 213. "A figure of Syntax is the intentional deviation in the usual construction of a word."—*Ib.*, 213. "Synecdoche is putting the name of the whole of anything for a part or a part for the whole."—*Ib.*, 215. "Apostrophe is turning off from the regular course of the subject to address some person or thing."—*Ib.*, 215. "Even young pupils will perform such exercises with surprising interest and facility, and will unconsciously gain, in a little time, more knowledge of the structure of Language than he can acquire by a drilling of several years in the usual routine of parsing."—*Ib., Preface*, p. iv. "A few Rules of construction are employed in this Part, to guide in the exercise of parsing."—*Ibidem.* "The name of every person, object, or thing, which can be thought of, or spoken of, is a noun."—*Ib.*, p. 18; *Abridged Ed.*, 19. "A dot, resembling our period, is used between every word, as well as at the close of the verses."—*W. Day's Punctuation*, p. 16; *London*, 1847. "Casting types in matrices was invented by Peter Schoeffer, in 1452."—*Ib.*, p. 23. "On perusing it, he said, that, so far from it showing the prisoner's guilt, it positively established his innocence."—*Ib.*, p. 37. "By printing the *nominative* and *verb* in *Italic* letters, the reader will be able to distinguish them at a glance."—*Ib.*, p. 77. "It is well, no doubt, to avoid using unnecessary words."—*Ib.*, p. 99. "Meeting a friend the other day, he said to me, 'Where are you going?'"—*Ib.*, p. 124. "John was first denied *apples*, then he was promised *them*, then he was offered *them*."—*Lennie's Gram.*, 5th Ed., p. 62. "He was denied admission."—*Wells's School Gram.*, 1st Ed., p. 146. "They were offered a pardon."—*Pond's Murray*, p. 118; *Wells*, 146. "I was this day shown a new potatoe."—DARWIN: *Webster's Philos. Gram.*, p. 179; *Imp. Gram.*, 128; *Frazee's Gram.*, 153; *Weld's*, 153. "Nouns or pronouns which denote males are of the masculine gender."—*S. S. Greene's Gram.*, 1st Ed., p. 211. "There are three degrees of comparison— the positive, comparative, and superlative."—*Ib.*, p. 216; *First Les.*, p. 49.

"The first two refer to direction; the third, to locality."—*Ib., Gr.,* p. 103. "The following are some of the verbs which take a direct and indirect object."—*Ib.,* p. 62. "I was not aware of his being the judge of the Supreme Court."—*Ib.,* p. 86. "An indirect question may refer to either of the five elements of a declarative sentence."—*Ib.,* p. 123. "I am not sure *that he will be present = of his being present.*"—*Ib.,* p. 169. "We left on Tuesday."—*Ib.,* p. 103. "He left, as he told me, before the arrival of the steamer."—*Ib.,* p. 143. "We told him *that he must leave* = We told him *to leave.*"—*Ib.,* p. 168. "Because he was unable to persuade the multitude, he left in disgust."—*Ib.,* p. 172. "He *left,* and *took* his brother with him."—*Ib.,* p. 254. "This stating, or declaring, or denying any thing, is called the indicative mode, or manner of speaking."—*Weld's Gram.,* 2d Ed., p. 72; *Abr. Ed.,* 59. "This took place at our friend Sir Joshua Reynold's."—*Weld's Gram.,* 2d Ed., p. 150; *Imp. Ed.,* 154. "The manner of a young lady's employing herself usefully in reading will be the subject of another paper."—*Ib.,* 150; or 154. "Very little time is necessary for Johnson's concluding a treaty with the bookseller."—*Ib.,* 150; or 154. "My father is not now sick, but if he *was* your services would be welcome."—*Chandler's Grammar,* 1821, p. 54. "When we begin to write or speak, we ought previously to fix in our minds a clear conception of the end to be aimed at."—*Blair's Rhetoric,* p. 193. "Length of days are in her right hand, and in her left hand riches and honor."—*Bullions's Analytical and Practical Grammar,* 1849, p. 59. "The active and passive present express different ideas."—*Ib.,* p. 235. "An *Improper Diphthong,* or Digraph, is a diphthong in which only one of the vowels are sounded."—*Fowler's E. Gram.,* 8vo, 1850, §115. "The real origin of the words are to be sought in the Latin."—*Ib.,* §120. "What sort of an alphabet the Gothic languages possess, we know; what sort of alphabet they require, we can determine."—*Ib.,* §127. "The Runic Alphabet whether borrowed or invented by the early Goths, is of greater antiquity than either the oldest Teutonic or the Moeso-Gothic Alphabets."—*Ib.,* §129. "Common to the

Masculine and the Neuter Genders."—*Ib.*, §222. "In the Anglo-Saxon *his* was common to both the Masculine and Neuter Genders."—*Ib.*, §222. "When time, number, or dimension are specified, the adjective follows the substantive."—*Ib.*, §459. "Nor pain, nor grief, nor anxious fear Invade thy bounds."—*Ib.*, §563. "To Brighton the Pavilion lends a *lath and plaster* grace."—*Ib.*, §590. "From this consideration nouns have been given but one person, the THIRD."—*D. C. Allen's Grammatic Guide*, p. 10.

"For it seems to guard and cherish
Even the wayward dreamer—I."—*Home Journal.*

EXAMPLES FOR PARSING.

PRAXIS XIII.—SYNTACTICAL.

In the following Lessons, are exemplified most of the Exceptions, some of the Notes, and many of the Observations, under the preceding Rules of Syntax; to which Exceptions, Notes, or Observations, the learner may recur, for an explanation of whatsoever is difficult in the parsing, or peculiar in the construction, of these examples or others.

LESSON I.—PROSE.

"*The* higher a bird flies, *the* more out of danger he is; and *the* higher a Christian soars above the world, *the* safer are his comforts."—*Sparke.*

"*In* this point of view, and *with* this explanation, *it* is supposed by some grammarians, that our language contains *a* few Impersonal Verbs; that is, *verbs* which declare the existence of some action or state, but *which* do not refer to any animate being, or any determinate particluar subject."—*L. Murray's Gram.*, 8vo, p. 109.

"Thus in England and France, a great landholder possesses *a hundred times* the property that is necessary for the subsistence of a family; and each landlord has perhaps *a* hundred families dependent on him for subsistence."—*Webster's Essays*, p. 87.

"*It* is as possible to become *pedantick* by fear of pedantry, as to be *troublesome* by ill timed civility."—*Johnson's Rambler*, No. 173.

"*To* commence *author, is* to claim praise; and no man can justly aspire to honour, but at the hazard of disgrace."—*Ib.*, No. 93.

"*For* ministers to be silent in the cause of Christ, *is* to renounce it; and to fly *is* to desert it."—SOUTH: *Crabb's Synonymes*, p. 7.

"Such instances shew how much *the sublime* depends upon a just selection of circumstances; and *with* how great care every circumstance must be avoided, which *by* bordering *in the least* upon *the mean*, or even upon *the gay* or *the trifling*, alters the tone of the emotion."—*Blair's Rhet.*, p. 43.

"This great poet and philosopher, *the* more *he* contemplated the nature of the Deity, *found* that *he* waded *but the* more out of his depth, and that *he* lost *himself* in the thought *instead* of finding an end to it."—*Addison.* "*Odin, which* in Anglo-Saxon was *Woden*, was the supreme god of the Goths, answering to the Jupiter of the Greeks."—*Webster's Essays*, p. 262.

"Because confidence, that *charm* and *cement* of intimacy, *is* wholly wanting in the intercourse."—*Opie, on Lying*, p. 146.

"Objects of hearing may be compared together, as also *of* taste, *of* smell, and *of* touch: but the chief *fund* of comparison *are objects* of sight."—*Kames, El. of Crit.*, Vol. ii, p. 136.

"The various relations of the various Objects exhibited by this (I mean relations of *near* and *distant, present* and *absent, same* and *different, definite* and *indefinite,* &c.) made it necessary that *here there* should not be one, but many Pronouns, such as *He, This, That, Other, Any, Some,* &c."—*Harris's Hermes,* p. 72.

"Mr. Pope's Ethical Epistles *deserve* to be mentioned with signal honour, *as* a *model,* next to *perfect, of* this kind of poetry."—*Blair's Rhet.,* p. 402.

"The knowledge *of why* they so exist, must be the last act of favour *which* time and toil will bestow."—*Rush, on the Voice,* p. 253.

"*It* is unbelief, and *not faith, that* sinks the sinner into despondency.—Christianity disowns such characters."—*Fuller, on the Gospel,* p. 141.

"That God created the universe, [and] that men are accountable for their actions, *are frequently mentioned* by logicians, as instances of the mind judging."

LESSON II.—PROSE.

"*To* censure works, *not men, is* the just *prerogative* of criticism, and accordingly all personal censure is here avoided, unless *where necessary* to illustrate some general proposition."—*Kames, El. of Crit., Introduction,* p. 27.

"*There remains* to show by examples the manner of treating subjects, so as to give them a ridiculous appearance."—*Ib.,* Vol. i, p. 303.

"The making of poetry, *like* any other *handicraft,* may be learned by industry."—*Macpherson's Preface to Ossian,* p. xiv.

"Whatever is found more strange or beautiful than *was expected*, is judged to be more strange or beautiful than it is in reality."—*Kames, El. of Crit.*, Vol. i, p. 243.

"Thus the body of an animal, and of a plant, *are composed* of certain great vessels; these[,] of *smaller*; and these again[,] of still *smaller*, without end, *as* far as we can discover."—*Id., ib.*, p. 270.

"This cause of beauty, is too extensive to be handled *as a branch* of any other subject: for *to* ascertain with accuracy even the proper meaning of words, *not to talk* of their figurative power, *would require* a large volume; *an* useful *work* indeed, but not to be attempted without a large stock of time, study, and reflection."—*Id.*, Vol. ii, p. 16.

"O the hourly *dangers* that we here walk *in*! Every sense, and member, *is* a snare; every creature, and every duty, *is* a snare to us."—*Baxter, Saints's Rest.*

"*For* a man *to give* his opinion of what he sees *but* in part, *is* an unjustifiable *piece* of rashness and folly."—*Addison.*

"*That* the sentiments thus prevalent among the early Jews *respecting* the divine authority of the Old Testament were correct, *appears* from the testimony of Jesus Christ and his apostles."—*Gurney's Essays*, p. 69.

"So in Society we are not our *own*, but Christ's, and the church's, to good works and services, yet all in love."—*Barclay's Works*, Vol. i, p. 84.

"He [*Dr. Johnson*] sat up in his bed, *clapped* his hands, *and cried*, 'O brave we!'—a peculiar *exclamation* of *his* when he rejoices."— *Boswell's Life of Johnson*, Vol. iii, p. 56.

"Single, double, and treble emphasis *are* nothing but examples of antithesis."—*Knowles's Elocutionist*, p. xxviii.

"The curious *thing, and what,* I would almost say, *settles* the point, *is,* that we do *Horace* no service, even according to our view of the matter, by rejecting the scholiast's explanation. No two eggs can be *more like each other* than Horace's *Malthinus* and Seneca's *Mecenas.*"— *Philological Museum*, Vol. i, p. 477. "*Acting, conduct, behaviour,* abstracted from all regard to what is, in fact and event, the consequence of *it, is itself* the natural object of this moral discernment, as speculative truth *and* [say *or*] falsehood is *of* speculative reason."—*Butler's Analogy*, p. 277.

"*To* do what is *right,* with unperverted faculties, *is* ten *times easier* than to undo what is wrong."—*Porter's Analysis*, p. 37.

"Some *natures the* more *pains* a man takes to reclaim them, *the* worse they are."—L'ESTRANGE: *Johnson's Dict., w. Pains.*

"Says *John Milton,* in that impassioned speech for the Liberty of Unlicensed Printing, where every word leaps with intellectual life, 'Who kills a man, *kills* a reasonable creature, God's image; but *who* destroys a good book, *kills* reason itself, kills the image of God, as it were, in the eye. Many a man lives a burden upon the earth; but a good book is the precious life-blood of a master spirit, embalmed and treasured up on purpose for a life beyond life!'"—*Louisville Examiner,* June, 1850.

LESSON III.—PROSE.

"The philosopher, the saint, or the hero—*the* wise, *the* good, or the great man—very often lies hid and concealed in a plebeian, *which* a proper education might have disinterred and *brought* to light."—*Addison.*

"The *year before*, he had so used the matter, that *what* by force, *what* by policy, he had taken from the Christians *above* thirty small castles."—*Knolles.*

"*It* is an important truth, that religion, vital *religion*, the *religion* of the heart, is the most powerful auxiliary of reason, in waging war with the passions, and promoting that sweet composure which constitutes the peace of God."—*Murray's Key*, p. 181.

"*Pray, sir, be pleased* to take the part of *us beauties* and *fortunes* into your consideration, and do not let us *be flattered* out of our senses. *Tell* people that *we* fair *ones* expect honest plain answers, as well as other folks."—*Spectator*, No. 534. "*Unhappy it* would be *for* us, *did* not uniformity *prevail* in morals: *that* our actions should uniformly be directed to what is *good* and against what is *ill*, is the greatest *blessing* in society; and *in* order to uniformity of action, uniformity of sentiment is indispensable."—*Kames, El. of Crit.,* Vol. ii, p. 366.

"Thus the pleasure of all the senses is *the same* in *all, high* and *low, learned* and *unlearned*."—*Burke, on Taste*, p. 39.

"*Upwards* of eight millions of acres *have*, I believe, been thus disposed of."—*Society in America*, Vol. i, p. 333.

"The Latin Grammar comes *something* nearer, but yet does not hit the mark *neither*."—*Johnson's Gram. Com.*, p. 281.

"*Of* the like nature is the following inaccuracy of *Dean Swift's*."—*Blair's Rhet.*, p. 105. "Thus, Sir, I have given *you* my own opinion, relating to this weighty affair, as well as *that* of a great majority of both houses here."—*Ib.*

"A foot is just *twelve* times as long as an *inch*; and an hour is sixty *times* the *length* of a minute."—*Murray's Gram.*, p. 48.

"What can we expect, who come *a gleaning*, not after the first reapers, but after the *very* beggars?"—*Cowley's Pref. to Poems*, p. x.

"In our *Lord's being betrayed* into the hands of the chief-priests and scribes, by Judas Iscariot; in *his being* by them *delivered* to the Gentiles; in *his being mocked, scourged, spitted on*, [say *spit upon*,] and *crucified*; and in his *rising* from the dead after three days; there was much that was singular, complicated, and not to be easily calculated on before hand."—*Gurney's Essays*, p. 40.

"To be *morose, implacable, inexorable*, and *revengeful*, is one of the greatest degeneracies of human nature."—*Dr. J. Owen.*

"Now, says *he*, if tragedy, which is in its nature *grand* and *lofty*, will not admit of this, *who can forbear laughing* to hear the historian Gorgias Leontinus styling Xerxes, that cowardly Persian king, *Jupiter*; and vultures, living *sepulchres*?"—*Holmes's Rhetoric?*, Part II, p. 14.

"O let thy all-seeing eye, and not the eye of the world, be the star to steer my course *by*; and let thy blessed favour, more than the liking of any sinful men, be ever my study and delight."—*Jenks's Prayers*, p. 156.

LESSON IV.—PROSE.

"O *the Hope* of Israel, *the Saviour thereof* in time of trouble, why *shouldest thou* be as a *stranger* in the land, and as a way-faring *man*, that turneth aside to tarry for a night?"—*Jeremiah*, xiv, 8.

"When once the long-suffering of God waited in the days of Noah, while the ark was *a preparing, wherein* few, *that* is, eight souls, were saved."—*1 Peter*, iii, 20.

"Mercy and truth *are* met together; righteousness and peace have kissed *each other*."—*Psalms*, lxxxv, 10.

"But *in vain* they do worship me, teaching for doctrines the commandments of men."—*Matt.*, xv, 9.

"Knowest thou not this *of old*, since man was placed upon the earth, that the *triumphing* of the *wicked* is short, and the joy of the hypocrite *but* for a moment?"—*Job*, xx, 4, 5.

"For now we *see* through a glass darkly; but *then, face* to *face*: now I *know* in part; but then shall I know even as also I am known."—*1 Cor.*, xiii, 12.

"For then the *king of Babylon's* army besieged Jerusalem: and Jeremiah the *Prophet* was shut up in the court of the prison which was in the *king of Judah's* house."—*Jer.*, xxxii, 2.

"For Herod had laid hold on John, and *bound* him, and *put* him in prison, for *Herodias'* sake, his *brother* Philip's *wife*."—*Matt.*, xiv, 3.

"And now I have sent a cunning man, endued with understanding, *of Huram* my *father's*, the *son* of a woman of the daughters of Dan."—*2 Chron.*, ii, 13.

"Bring no *more* vain oblations: incense is an abomination unto me; the new moons and sabbaths, the *calling* of assemblies, I *cannot away with: it* is iniquity *even* the solemn *meeting*."—*Isaiah*, i, 13.

"For I have heard the voice of the daughter of Zion, that bewaileth herself, that spreadeth her hands, *saying,* Woe is *me* now! for my soul is wearied *because* of murderers."—*Jer.,* iv, 31.

"She saw men portrayed upon the wall, the *images* of the Chaldeans portrayed with vermilion, girded with girdles upon their loins, exceeding in dyed attire upon their heads, all of them princes *to* look *to, after* the manner of the Babylonians of Chaldea, the *land* of their nativity."—*Ezekiel,* xxiii, 15.

"And on them *was written* according to all the words which the Lord spake with you in the mount, out of the midst of the fire, in the day of the assembly."—*Deut.,* ix, 10.

"And he charged them that they *should tell no man*: but *the* more he charged them, so much *the* more a great *deal* they published it."—*Mark,* vii, 36.

"The results which God has connected with actions, will inevitably occur, all the created *power* in the universe to the contrary *notwithstanding*."—*Wayland's Moral Science*, p. 5.

"Am *I* not an *apostle*? am *I* not *free*? have I not seen Jesus Christ our Lord? are not *ye* my *work* in the Lord? If I be not an apostle unto others, yet doubtless I am *to* you; for the *seal* of *mine* apostleship are *ye* in the Lord."—*1 Cor.,* ix, 1, 2.

"Not *to insist* upon this, *it* is evident, that formality is a term of general import. It implies, that in religious exercises of all kinds *the* outward and [the] inward man *are* at diametrical variance."—*Chapman's Sermons to Presbyterians*, p. 354.

LESSON V.—VERSE.

"*See* the sole bliss Heaven *could* on all *bestow,*
Which *who but* feels, can taste, *but* thinks, can know;
Yet, poor with fortune, and with learning blind,
The bad must miss, *the good*, untaught, will find."—*Pope.*

"There *are, who, deaf* to mad Ambition's call,
Would shrink to hear th' obstreperous trump of fame;
Supremely *blest,* if to their portion fall
Health, competence, and peace."—*Beattie.*

"High stations *tumult,* but *not bliss,* create;
None think *the great* unhappy, but *the great.*
Fools gaze and *envy*: envy darts a sting,
Which makes a swain as *wretched* as a king."—*Young.*

"Lo, earth receives him from the bending skies!
Sink down, *ye mountains*; and, *ye valleys, rise*;
With heads declin'd, *ye cedars,* homage *pay*;
Be smooth, *ye rocks; ye* rapid *floods, give* way."—*Pope.*

"Amid the forms which this full world presents
Like rivals to his choice, what human breast
E'er doubts, before the *transient and minute,*
To prize the *vast,* the *stable,* and *sublime*?"—*Akenside.*

"Now fears in dire vicissitude invade;
The rustling brake *alarms,* and quiv'ring *shade*:
Nor light nor darkness brings his *pain* relief;
One shows the plunder, and one hides the thief."—*Johnson.*

"If Merab's choice could have complied with *mine*,
Merab, my elder comfort, had been *thine*:
And *hers*, at *last*, should have with *mine* complied,
Had I not *thine* and Michael's heart descried."—*Cowley*.

"The people have *as much* a negative voice
To hinder *making* war without their choice,
As kings of making laws in parliament:
'*No money*' *is* as *good* as '*No assent*.'"—*Butler*.

"Full *many a gem* of purest ray serene
The dark unfathom'd caves of ocean bear;
Full *many a flower* is born to blush unseen,
And waste its sweetness on the desert air."—*Gray*.

"*Oh fool*! to think God hates the worthy *mind*,
The lover and the love of human kind,
Whose life is healthful, and *whose* conscience clear,
Because *he* wants *a* thousand pounds *a* year."—*Pope*.

"O *Freedom*! sovereign *boon* of Heav'n,
Great *charter*, with our being given;
For *which* the patriot and the sage
Have plann'd, have bled thro' ev'ry age!"—*Mallet*.

LESSON VI.—VERSE.

"Am I to set my life upon a throw,
Because a bear is rude and surly? *No*."—*Cowper*.

"*Poor, guiltless I*! and can I choose but *smile*,
When every coxcomb knows me by my style?"—*Pope*.

"Remote from man, with God he pass'd his days,
Prayer all his *business*, all his *pleasure praise*."—*Parnell.*

"These are *thy* blessings, *Industry*! rough power;
Whom labour still attends, and *sweat*, and *pain*."—*Thomson.*

"*What ho! thou genius* of the clime, *what ho!*
Liest thou *asleep* beneath these hills of snow?"—*Dryden.*

"*What*! canst thou not forbear me *half an hour*?
Then *get* thee gone, and *dig* my grave thyself."—*Shak.*

"Then palaces and lofty domes arose;
These for devotion, and for pleasure *those*."—*Blackmore.*

"'Tis very dangerous, *tampering* with a muse;
The profit's small, and you have much to lose."—*Roscommon.*

"*Lucretius English'd*! 't was a work *might shake*
The power of English verse to undertake."—*Otway.*

"*The best* may slip, and *the* most *cautious fall*;
He's *more* than *mortal*, that ne'er err'd *at all*."—*Pomfret.*

"*Poets* large *souls* heaven's noblest stamps do bear,
Poets, the watchful angels' darling care."—*Stepney.*

"Sorrow breaks reasons, and reposing hours;
Makes the night *morning*, and the noon-tide *night*."—*Shak.*

"Nor then the solemn nightingale *ceas'd warbling*."—*Milton.*

"And O, poor hapless *nightingale*, thought I,
How *sweet* thou singst, how *near* the deadly *snare*!"—*Id.*

"He calls for *famine*, and the meagre fiend
Blows mildew *from between his* shrivell'd lips."—*Cowper*.

"If o'er their lives a refluent *glance* they cast,
Theirs is *the present* who can praise *the past*."—*Shenstone*.

"Who wickedly is *wise*, or madly *brave*,
Is but the more a fool, the *more* a knave."—*Pope*.

"Great *eldest-born* of Dullness, blind and bold!
Tyrant! more cruel than Procrustes old;
Who, to his iron bed, by torture, fits,
Their nobler *part*, the *souls* of suffering wits."—*Mallet*.

"Parthenia, *rise.*—What voice alarms my ear?
Away. Approach not. Hah! *Alexis* there!"—*Gay*.

"Nor is it *harsh* to make, nor *hard* to find
A country *with—ay*, or without mankind."—*Byron*.

"A *frame* of adamant, a *soul* of fire,
No dangers fright him, and *no* labours tire."—*Johnson*.

"Now *pall* the tasteless *meats*, and joyless *wines*,
And *luxury* with sighs *her slave resigns*."—*Id*.

"*Seems?* madam; nay, it is: I know not *seems*—
For I have that within which passes show."—*Hamlet*.

"*Return? said* Hector, fir'd with stern disdain:
What! coop whole armies in our walls again?"—*Pope*.

"He whom the fortune of the field shall cast
From forth his chariot, *mount* the next in haste."—*Id.*

"*Yet here, Laertes? aboard, aboard, for* shame!"—*Shak.*

"*Justice*, most gracious *Duke; O grant me* justice!"—*Id.*

"But what a *vengeance* makes thee *fly*
From me too, as thine enemy?"—*Butler.*

"Immortal *Peter*! first of monarchs! He
His stubborn *country* tam'd, *her* rocks, *her* fens,
Her floods, *her* seas, *her* ill-submitting sons."—*Thomson.*

"O arrogance! Thou liest, thou thread, thou thimble,
Thou yard, three-quarters, half-yard, quarter, nail,
Thou flea, thou nit, thou winter-cricket, thou:—
Brav'd in mine own house with a skein of thread!
Away, thou rag, thou quantity, thou remnant;
Or I shall so be-mete thee with thy yard,
As thou shalt think on prating whilst thou liv'st."
　　SHAK.: *Taming of the Shrew,* Act IV, Sc 3.

GENERAL REVIEW.

This twelfth chapter of Syntax is devoted to a series of lessons, methodically digested, wherein are reviewed and reapplied, mostly in the order of the parts of speech, all those syntactical principles heretofore given which are useful for the correction of errors.

IMPROPRIETIES FOR CORRECTION.

FALSE SYNTAX FOR A GENERAL REVIEW.

[Fist][The following examples of false syntax are arranged for a General Review of the doctrines contained in the preceding Rules and Notes. Being nearly all of them exact quotations, they are also a sort of syllabus of verbal criticism on the various works from which they are taken. What corrections they are supposed to need, may be seen by inspection of the twelfth chapter of the Key. It is here expected, that by recurring to the instructions before given, the learner who takes them as an oral exercise, will ascertain for himself the proper form of correcting each example, according to the particular Rule or Note under which it belongs. When two or more errors occur in the same example, they ought to be corrected successively, in their order. The erroneous sentence being read aloud as it stands, the pupil should say, "*first*, Not proper, because, &c." And when the first error has thus been duly corrected by a brief and regular syllogism, either the same pupil or an other should immediately proceed, and say, "*Secondly,* Not proper *again,* because," &c. And so of the third error, and the fourth, if there be so many. In this manner, a class may be taught to speak in succession without any waste of time, and, after some practice, with a near approach to the PERFECT ACCURACY which is the great end of grammatical instruction. When time cannot be allowed for this regular exercise, these examples may still be profitably rehearsed by a more rapid process, one pupil reading aloud the quoted false grammar, and an other responding to each example, by reading the intended correction from the Key.]

LESSON I.—ARTICLES.

"And they took stones, and made an heap."—*Com. Bibles; Gen.,* xxxi, 46. "And I do know a many fools, that stand in better place."—*Beauties of Shak.,* p. 44. "It is a strong antidote to the turbulence of passion, and violence of pursuit."—*Kames, El. of Crit.,* Vol. i, p. xxiii. "The word *news* may admit of either a singular or plural application."—*Wright's Gram.,* p. 39. "He has earned a fair and a honorable reputation."—*Ib.,* p. 140. "There are two general forms, called the solemn and familiar style."—*Sanborn's Gram.,* p. 109. "Neither the article nor preposition may be omitted."—*Wright's Gram.,* p 190. "A close union is also observable between the Subjunctive and Potential Moods."—*Ib.,* p. 72. "We should render service, equally, to a friend, neighbour, and an enemy."—*Ib.,* p. 140. "Till an habit is obtained of aspirating strongly."—*Sheridan's Elocution,* p. 49. "There is an uniform, steady use of the same signs."—*Ib.,* p. 163. "A traveller remarks the most objects he sees."—*Jamieson's Rhet.,* p. 72. "What is the name of the river on which London stands? The Thames."—"We sometimes find the last line of a couplet or triplet stretched out to twelve syllables."—*Adam's Lat. and Eng. Gram.,* p. 282. "Nouns which follow active verbs, are not in the nominative case."—*Blair's Gram.,* p. 14. "It is a solemn duty to speak plainly of wrongs, which good men perpetrate."—*Channing's Emancip.*, p. 71. "Gathering of riches is a pleasant torment."—*Treasury of Knowledge, Dict.*, p. 446. "It [the lamentation of Helen for Hector] is worth the being quoted."—*Coleridge's Introd.*, p. 100. "*Council* is a noun which admits of a singular and plural form."—*Wright's Gram.*, p. 137. "To exhibit the connexion between the Old and the New Testaments."—*Keith's Evidences*, p. 25. "An apostrophe discovers the omission of a letter or letters."—*Guy's Gram*, p. 95. "He is immediately ordained, or rather acknowledged an hero."—*Pope, Preface to the Dunciad.* "Which is the same in both the leading and following State."—*Brightland's Gram.*, p. 86. "Pronouns, as will be seen hereafter, have a distinct nominative, possessive, and objective case."—*Blair's Gram.*, p. 15. "A word of many syllables is called polysyllable."—*Beck's Outline of E. Gram.*, p. 4. "Nouns have two numbers, singular and plural."—*Ib.*, p. 6. "They have three genders, masculine, feminine, and neuter."—*Ib.*, p. 6. "They have three cases, nominative, possessive, and objective."—*Ib.*, p. 6. "Personal Pronouns have, like Nouns, two numbers, singular and plural. Three genders, masculine, feminine, and neuter. Two cases, nominative and objective."—*Ib.*, p. 10. "He must be wise enough to know the singular from plural."—*Ib.*, p. 20. "Though they may be able to meet the every reproach which any one of their fellows may prefer."—*Chalmers, Sermons*, p. 104. "Yet for love's sake I rather beseech thee, being such an one as Paul the aged."—*Ep. to Philemon*, 9. "Being such one as Paul the aged."—*Dr. Webster's Bible.* "A people that jeoparded their lives unto the death."—*Judges*, v, 18. "By preventing the too great accumulation of seed within a too narrow compass."—*The Friend*, Vol. vii, p. 97. "Who fills up the middle space between the animal and intellectual nature, the visible and invisible world."—*Addison, Spect.*, No. 519. "The Psalms abound with instances of an harmonious arrangement of the words."—*Murray's Gram.*, Vol. i, p. 339. "On another table were an ewer and vase, likewise of gold."—*N. Y. Mirror,* xi, 307. "*Th* is said to have two sounds sharp, and flat."—*Wilson's Essay on Gram.*, p. 33. "Section (§) is used in subdividing of a chapter into lesser parts."—*Brightland's Gram.*, p. 152. "Try it in a Dog or an Horse or any other Creature."—*Locke, on Ed.*, p. 46. "But particularly in learning of Languages there is least occasion for poseing of Children."—*Ib.*, p. 296. "What kind of a noun is *river*, and why?"—*Smith's New Gram.*, p. 10. "Is *William's* a proper or common noun?"—*Ib.*, p. 12. "What kind of an article, then, shall we call *the*?"—*Ib.*, p. 13.

"Each burns alike, who can, or cannot write,
Or with a rival's or an eunuch's spite."—*Pope, on Crit.*, l. 30.

LESSON II.—NOUNS, OR CASES.

"And there is stamped upon their Imaginations Idea's that follow them with Terror and Affrightment."—*Locke, on Ed.*, p. 251. "There's not a wretch that lives on common charity, but's happier than me."—VENICE PRESERVED: *Kames, El. of Crit.*, i, 63. "But they overwhelm whomsoever is ignorant of them."—*Common School Journal*, i,115. "I have received a letter from my cousin, she that was here last week."—*Inst.*, p. 129. "Gentlemens Houses are seldom without Variety of Company."—*Locke, on Ed.*, p. 107. "Because Fortune has laid them below the level of others, at their Masters feet."—*Ib.*, p. 221. "We blamed neither John nor Mary's delay."—*Nixon's Parser*, p. 117. "The book was written by Luther the reformer's order."—*Ib.*, p. 59. "I saw on the table of the saloon Blair's Sermons, and somebody else (I forget who's) sermons, and a set of noisy children."—*Lord Byron's Letters*. "Or saith he it altogether for our sakes?"—*1 Cor.*, ix, 10. "He was not aware of the duke's being his competitor."—*Sanborn's Gram.*, p. 190. "It is no condition of a word's being an adjective, that it must be placed before a noun."—FOWLE: *ib.*, p.

190. "Though their Reason corrected the wrong Idea's they had taken in."—*Locke, on Ed.*, p. 251. "It was him, who taught me to hate slavery."—*Morris, in Congress*, 1839. "It is him and his kindred, who live upon the labour of others."—*Id., ib.* "Payment of Tribute is an Acknowledgment of his being King to whom we think it Due."—*Right of Tythes*, p. 161. "When we comprehend what we are taught."—*Ingersoll's Gram.*, p. 14. "The following words, and parts of words, must be taken notice of."—*Priestley's Gram.*, p. 96. "Hence tears and commiseration are so often made use of."—*Blair's Rhet.*, p. 269. "JOHN-A-NOKES, *n. s.* A fictitious name, made use of in law proceedings."—*Chalmers, Eng. Dict.* "The construction of Matter, and Part taken hold of."—*B. F. Fisk's Greek Gram.*, p. x. "And such other names, as carry with them the Idea's of some thing terrible and hurtful."—*Locke, on Ed.*, p. 250. "Every learner then would surely be glad to be spared the trouble and fatigue"—*Pike's Hebrew Lexicon*, p. iv. "'Tis not the owning ones Dissent from another, that I speak against."—*Locke, on Ed.*, p 265. "A man that cannot Fence will be more careful to keep out of Bullies and Gamesters Company, and will not be half so apt to stand upon Punctilio's."—*Ib.*, p. 357. "From such Persons it is, one may learn more in one Day, than in a Years rambling from one Inn to another."—*Ib.*, p. 377. "A long syllable is generally considered to be twice the length of a short one."—*Blair's Gram.*, p. 117. "*I* is of the first person, and singular number; *Thou* is second per. sing.; *He, She*, or *It*, is third per. sing.; *We* is first per. plural; *Ye* or *You* is second per. plural; *They* is third per. plural."—*Kirkham's Gram.*, p. 46. "This actor, doer, or producer of the action, is the nominative."—*Ib.*, p. 43. "No Body can think a Boy of Three or Seven Years old, should be argued with, as a grown Man."—*Locke, on Ed.*, p. 129. "This was in one of the Pharisees' houses, not, in Simon the leper's."—*Hammond.* "Impossible! it can't be me."—*Swift.* "Whose grey top shall tremble, Him descending."—*Dr. Bentley.* "What gender is *woman*, and why?"—*Smith's New Gram.*, p. 8. "What gender, then, is *man*, and why?"—

Ibid. "Who is *I*; who do you mean when you say *I?*"—*R. W. Green's Gram.*, p. 19. "It [Parnassus] is a pleasant air, but a barren soil."—*Locke, on Ed.*, p. 311. "You may, in three days time, go from Galilee to Jerusalem."—*Josephus*, Vol. 5, p. 174. "And that which is left of the meat-offering shall be Aaron's and his sons."—SCOTT'S BIBLE, and BRUCE'S: *Lev.*, ii, 10. See also ii, 3.

"For none in all the world, without a lie,
Can say that this is mine, excepting I."—*Bunyan.*

LESSON III.—ADJECTIVES

"When he can be their Remembrancer and Advocate every Assises and Sessions."—*Right of Tythes*, p. 244. "Doing, denotes all manner of action; as, to dance, to play, to write, to read, to teach, to fight, &c."—*Buchanan's Gram.*, p. 33. "Seven foot long,"—"eight foot long,"—"fifty foot long."—*Walker's Particles*, p. 205. "Nearly the whole of this twenty-five millions of dollars is a dead loss to the nation."—*Fowler, on Tobacco*, p. 16. "Two negatives destroy one another."—*R. W. Green's Gram.*, p. 92. "We are warned against excusing sin in ourselves, or in each other."—*The Friend*, iv, 108. "The Russian empire is more extensive than any government in the world."—*School Geog.* "You will always have the Satisfaction to think it the Money of all other the best laid out."—*Locke, on Ed.*, p. 145. "There is no one passion which all mankind so naturally give into as pride."—*Steele, Spect.*, No. 462. "O, throw away the worser part of it."—*Beauties of Shak.*, p 237. "He showed us a more agreeable and easier way."—*Inst.*, p. 134. "And the four last [are] to point out those further improvements."—*Jamieson's Rhet.*, p. 52; *Campbell's*, 187. "Where he has not distinct and, different clear Idea's."—*Locke, on Ed.*, p. 353. "Oh, when shall we have such another Rector of Laracor!"—*Hazlitt's Lect.* "Speech must have been absolutely necessary previous to the formation of society."—*Jamieson's Rhet.*, p. 2. "Go and tell them boys to be still."—*Inst.*, p. 135. "Wrongs are engraved on marble; benefits, on sand: these are apt to be requited; those, forgot."—*B.* "Neither of these several interpretations is the true one."—*B.* "My friend indulged himself in some freaks unbefitting the gravity of a clergyman."—*B.* "And their Pardon is All that either of their Impropriators will have to plead."—*Right of Tythes*, p. 196. "But the time usually chosen to send young Men abroad, is, I think, of all other, that which renders them least capable of reaping those Advantages."—*Locke, on Ed.*, p. 372. "It is a mere figment of the human imagination, a rhapsody of the transcendent unintelligible."—*Jamieson's Rhet.*, p. 120. "It contains a greater assemblage of sublime ideas, of bold and daring figures, than is perhaps any where to be met with."—*Blair's Rhet.*, p. 162. "The order in which the two last words are placed, should have been reversed."—*Ib.*, p. 204. "The *orders* in which the two last words are placed, should have been reversed."—*Murray's Gram.*, 8vo, p. 310. "In Demosthenes, eloquence *shown* forth with higher splendour, than perhaps in any that ever bore the name of an orator."—*Blair's Rhet.*, p. 242. "The circumstance of his being poor is decidedly favorable."— *Student's Manual*, p. 286. "The temptations to dissipation are greatly lessened by his being poor."—*Ib.*, p. 287. "For with her death that tidings came."—*Beauties of Shak.*, p. 257. "The next objection is, that these sort of authors are poor."—*Cleland.* "Presenting Emma as Miss Castlemain to these acquaintance."—*Opie's Temper.* "I doubt not but it will please more than the opera."—*Spect.*, No. 28. "The world knows only two, that's Rome and I."—*Ben Jonson.* "I distinguish these two things from one another."—*Blair's Rhet.*, p. 29. "And in this case, mankind reciprocally claim, and allow indulgence to each other."—*Sheridan's Lect.*, p. 29. "The six last books are said not to have received the finishing hand of the author."—*Blair's Rhet.*, p. 438. "The best executed part of the work, is the first six books."—*Ib.*, p. 447.

"To reason how can we be said to rise?
So many cares attend the being wise."—*Sheffield.*

LESSON IV.—PRONOUNS.

"Once upon a time a goose fed its young by a pond side."—*Goldsmith's Essays*, p. 175. "If either [work] have a sufficient degree of merit to recommend them to the attention of the public."—*Walker's Rhyming Dict.*, p. iii. "Now W. Mitchell his deceit is very remarkable."—*Barclay's Works*, i, 264 "My brother, I did not put the question to thee, for that I doubted of the truth of your belief."—*Bunyan's P. P.*, p. 158. "I had two elder brothers, one of which was a lieutenant-colonel."—*Robinson Crusoe*, p. 2. "Though *James* is here the object of the action, yet, he is in the nominative case."—*Wright's Gram.*, p. 64. "Here, *John* is the actor; and is known to be the nominative, by its answering to the question, 'Who struck Richard?'"—*Ib.*, p. 43. "One of the most distinguished privileges which Providence has conferred on mankind, is the power of communicating their thoughts to one another."—*Blair's Rhet.*, p. 9. "With some of the most refined feelings which belong to our frame."—*Ib.*, p. 13. "And the same instructions which assist others in composing, will assist them in judging of, and relishing, the beauties of composition."—*Ib.*, p. 12. "To overthrow all which had been yielded in favour of the army."—*Mrs. Macaulay's Hist.*, i, 335. "Let your faith stand in the Lord God who changes not, and that created all, and gives the increase of all."—*Friends' Advices*, 1676. "For it is, in truth, the sentiment or passion, which lies under the figured expression, that gives it any merit."—*Blair's Rhet.*, p. 133. "Verbs are words which affirm the being, doing, or suffering of a thing, together with the time it happens."—*Al. Murray's Gram.*, p. 29. "The Byass will always hang on that side, that nature first placed it."—*Locke, on Ed.*, p. 177. "They should be brought to do the things are fit for them."—*Ib.*, p. 178. "Various sources whence the

English language is derived."—*Murray's Gram.*, Vol. ii, p. 286. "This attention to the several cases, when it is proper to omit and when to redouble the copulative, is of considerable importance."—*Blair's Rhet.*, p. 113. "Cicero, for instance, speaking of the cases where killing another is lawful in self defence, uses the following words."—*Ib.*, p. 156. "But there is no nation, hardly any person so phlegmatic, as not to accompany their words with some actions and gesticulations, on all occasions, when they are much in earnest."—*Ib.*, p. 335. "*William's* is said to be governed by *coat*, because it follows *William's*"—*Smith's New Gram.*, p. 12. "There are many occasions in life, in which silence and simplicity are true wisdom."—*Murray's Key,* ii, 197. "In choosing umpires, the avarice of whom is excited."—*Nixon's Parser*, p. 153. "The boroughs sent representatives, which had been enacted."—*Ib.*, p. 154. "No man believes but what there is some order in the universe."—*Anon.* "The moon is orderly in her changes, which she could not be by accident."—*Id.* "Of Sphynx her riddles, they are generally two kinds."—*Bacons Wisdom*, p. 73. "They must generally find either their Friends or Enemies in Power."—*Brown's Estimate*, Vol. ii, p. 166. "For of old, every one took upon them to write what happened in their own time."—*Josephus's Jewish War, Pref.*, p. 4. "The Almighty cut off the family of Eli the high priest, for its transgressions."—See *Key.* "The convention then resolved themselves into a committee of the whole."—*Inst.*, p. 146. "The severity with which this denomination was treated, appeared rather to invite than to deter them from flocking to the colony."—*H. Adams's View*, p. 71. "Many Christians abuse the Scriptures and the traditions of the apostles, to uphold things quite contrary to it."—*Barclay's Works*, i, 461. "Thus, a circle, a square, a triangle, or a hexagon, please the eye, by their regularity, as beautiful figures."—*Blair's Rhet.*, p. 46. "Elba is remakable [sic—KTH] for its being the place to which Bonaparte was banished in 1814."—See *Sanborn's Gram.*, p. 190. "The editor has the reputation of his being a good linguist and critic."—See *ib.* "'Tis a Pride should be cherished in them."—*Locke, on Ed.*, p. 129. "And to restore us the Hopes of Fruits, to reward our Pains in its season."—*Ib.*, p. 136. "The comick representation of Death's victim relating its own tale."—*Wright's Gram.*, p. 103. "As for Scioppius his Grammar, that doth wholly concern the Latin Tongue."—DR. WILKINS: *Tooke's D. P.*, i, 7.

"And chiefly thee, O Spirit, who dost prefer
Before all temples the upright heart and pure,
Instruct me, for thou knowest."—*Bucke's Classical Gram.*, p. 45.

LESSON V.—VERBS.

"And there was in the same country shepherds, abiding in the field."—SCOTT'S BIBLE: *Luke*, ii. 8. "Whereof every one bear twins."—COM. BIBLE: *Sol. Song*, iv, 2. "Whereof every one bare twins."—ALGER'S BIBLE: *ib.* "Whereof every one beareth twins."—SCOTT'S BIBLE: *ib.* "He strikes out of his nature one of the most divine principles, that is planted in it."—*Addison, Spect.*, No. 181. "*Genii*, denote ærial spirits."—*Wright's Gram.*, p. 40. "In proportion as the long and large prevalence of such corruptions have been obtained by force."—BP. HALIFAX: *Brier's Analogy*, p. xvi. "Neither of these are fix'd to a Word of a general Signification, or proper Name."—*Brightland's Gram.*, p. 95. "Of which a few of the opening lines is all I shall give."—*Moore's Life of Byron.* "The riches we had in England was the slow result of long industry and wisdom."—DAVENANT: *Webster's Imp. Gram.*, p. 21; *Phil. Gram.*, 29. "The following expression appears to be correct:—'Much publick thanks *is* due.'"—*Wright's Gram.*, p. 201. "He hath been enabled to correct many mistakes."—*Lowth's Gram.*, p. x. "Which road takest thou here?"—*Ingersoll's Gram.*, p. 106. "Learnest thou thy lesson?"—*Ib.*, p. 105. "Learned they their pieces perfectly?"—*Ibid.* "Thou learnedst thy task well."—*Ibid.* "There are some can't relish the town, and others can't away with the country."—WAY OF THE WORLD: *Kames, El. of Crit.*, i, 304. "If thou meetest them, thou must put on an intrepid mien."—*Neef's Method of Ed.*, p. 201. "Struck with terror, as if Philip was something more than human."—*Blair's Rhet.*, p. 265. "If the personification of the form of Satan was admissible, it should certainly have been masculine."—*Jamieson's Rhet.*, p. 176. "If only one follow, there seems to be a defect in the sentence."—*Priestley's Gram.*, p. 104. "Sir, if thou have borne him hence, tell me where thou hast laid him."—*John*, xx, 15. "Blessed be the people that know the joyful sound."—*Psalms*, lxxxix, 15. "Every auditory take in good part those marks of respect and awe, which are paid them by one who addresses them."—*Blair's Rhet.*, p. 308. "Private causes were still pleaded [in the forum]: but the public was no longer interested; nor any general attention drawn to what passed there."—*Ib.*, p. 249. "Nay, what evidence can be brought to show, that the Inflection of the Classic tongues were not originally formed out of obsolete auxiliary words?"—*Murray's Gram.*, i, p. 112. "If the student reflects, that the principal and the auxiliary forms but one verb, he will have little or no difficulty, in the proper application of the present rule."—*Ib.*, p. 183. "For the sword of the enemy and fear is on every side."—*Jeremiah*, vi, 26. "Even the Stoics agree that nature and certainty is very hard to come at."—*Collier's Antoninus*, p. 71. "His politeness and obliging behaviour was changed."—*Priestley's Gram.*, p. 186. "His politeness and obliging behaviour were changed."—*Hume's Hist.*, Vol. vi, p. 14. "War and its honours was their employment and ambition."—*Goldsmith*. "Does *a* and *an* mean the same thing?"—*R. W. Green's Gram.*, p. 15. "When a number of words *come* in between the discordant parts, the ear does not detect the error."—*Cobbett's Gram.*, ¶ 185. "The sentence should be, 'When a number of words *comes* in,' &c."—*Wright's Gram.*, p. 170. "The nature of our language, the accent and pronunciation of it, inclines us to contract even all our regular verbs."—*Lowth's Gram.*, p. 45.

"The nature of our language, together with the accent and pronunciation of it, incline us to contract even all our Regular Verbs."—*Hiley's Gram.*, p. 45. "Prompt aid, and not promises, are what we ought to give."—*Author*. "The position of the several organs therefore, as well as their functions are ascertained."—*Medical Magazine*, 1833, p. 5. "Every private company, and almost every public assembly, afford opportunities of remarking the difference between a just and graceful, and a faulty and unnatural elocution."—*Enfield's Speaker*, p. 9. "Such submission, together with the active principle of obedience, make up the temper and character in us which answers to his sovereignty."— *Butler's Analogy*, p. 126. "In happiness, as in other things, there is a false and a true, an imaginary and a real."—*Fuller, on the Gospel*, p. 134. "To confound things that differ, and to make a distinction where there is no difference, is equally unphilosophical."—*Author*.

"I know a bank whereon the wild thyme blows,
  Where ox-lips and the nodding violet grows."—*Beaut. of Shak.*, p. 51.

LESSON VI.—VERBS.

"Whose business or profession prevent their attendance in the morning."—*Ogilby.* "And no church or officer have power over one another."—LECHFORD: *in Hutchinson's Hist.*, i, 373. "While neither reason nor experience are sufficiently matured to protect them."—*Woodbridge.* "Among the Greeks and Romans, every syllable, or the far greatest number at least, was known to have a fixed and determined quantity."—*Blair's Rhet.*, p. 383. "Among the Greeks and Romans, every syllable, or at least by far the greatest number of syllables, was known to have a fixed and determined quantity."—*Jamieson's Rhet.*, p. 303. "Their vanity is awakened and their passions exalted by the irritation, which their self-love receives from contradiction."—*Influence of Literature*, Vol. ii. p. 218. "I and he was neither of us any great swimmer."—*Anon.* "Virtue, honour, nay, even self-interest, *conspire* to recommend the measure."—*Murray's Gram.*, Vol. i, p. 150. "A correct plainness, and elegant simplicity, is the proper character of an introduction."—*Blair's Rhet.*, p. 308. "In syntax there is what grammarians call concord or agreement, and government."—*Infant School Gram.*, p. 128. "People find themselves able without much study to write and speak the English intelligibly, and thus have been led to think rules of no utility."— *Webster's Essays*, p. 6. "But the writer must be one who has studied to inform himself well, who has pondered his subject with care, and addresses himself to our judgment, rather than to our imagination."—*Blair's Rhet.*, p. 353. "But practice hath determined it otherwise; and has, in all the languages with which we are much acquainted, supplied the place of an interrogative mode, either by particles of interrogation, or by a peculiar order of the words in the sentence."—*Lowth's Gram.*, p. 84. "If the Lord have stirred thee up against me, let him accept an offering."—*1 Sam.*, xxvi, 19. "But if the priest's daughter be a widow, or divorced, and have no child, and is returned unto her father's house, as in her youth, she shall eat of her father's meat."—*Levit.*, xxii, 13. "Since we never have, nor ever shall study your sublime productions."—*Neef's Sketch*, p. 62. "Enabling us to form more distinct images of objects, than can be done with the utmost attention where these particulars are not found."—*Kames, El. of Crit.*, Vol. i, p. 174. "I hope you will consider what is spoke comes from my love."—*Shak.*, *Othello.* "We will then perceive how the designs of emphasis may be marred,"—*Rush, on the Voice*, p. 406. "I knew it was Crab, and goes me to the fellow that whips the dogs."—SHAK: *Joh. Dict., w.* ALE. "The youth was being consumed by a slow malady."—*Wright's Gram.*, p. 192. "If all men thought, spoke, and wrote alike, something resembling a perfect adjustment of these points may be accomplished."— *Ib.*, p. 240. "If you will replace what has been long since expunged from the language."—*Campbell's Rhet.*, p. 167; *Murray's Gram.*, i, 364. "As in all those faulty instances, I have now been giving."—*Blair's Rhet.*, p. 149. "This mood has also been improperly used in the following places."—*Murray's Gram.*, i, 184. "He [Milton] seems to have been well acquainted with his own genius, and to know what it was that nature had bestowed upon him."—*Johnson's Life of Milton.* "Of which I already gave one instance, the worst, indeed, that occurs in all the poem."—*Blair's Rhet.*, p. 395. "It is strange he never commanded you to have done it."—*Anon.* "History painters would have found it difficult, to have invented such a species of beings."—ADDISON: see *Lowth's Gram.*, p. 87. "Universal Grammar cannot be taught abstractedly, it must be done with reference to some language already known."—*Lowth's Preface*, p. viii. "And we might imagine, that if verbs had been so contrived, as simply to express these, no more was needful."—*Blair's Rhet.*, p. 82. "To a writer of such a genius as Dean Swift, the plain style was most admirably fitted."—*Ib.*, p. 181. "Please excuse my son's absence."—*Inst.*, p. 188. "Bid the boys to come in immediately."—*Ib.*

"Gives us the secrets of his Pagan hell,
  Where ghost with ghost in sad communion dwell."
    —*Crabbe's Bor.*, p. 306.

"Alas! nor faith, nor valour now remain;
  Sighs are but wind, and I must bear my chain."
    —*Walpole's Catal.*, p. 11.

LESSON VII.—PARTICIPLES.

"Of which the Author considers himself, in compiling the present work, as merely laying of the foundation-stone."—*Blair's Gram.*, p. ix. "On the raising such lively and distinct images as are here described."—*Kames, El. of Crit.*, i, 89. "They are necessary to the avoiding Ambiguities."—*Brightland's Gram.*, p. 95. "There is no neglecting it without falling into a dangerous error."—*Burlamaqui, on Law*, p. 41. "The contest resembles Don Quixote's fighting windmills."—*Webster's Essays*, p. 67. "That these verbs associate with verbs in all the tenses, is no proof of their having no particular time of their own."—*Murray's Gram.*, i, 190. "To justify my not following the tract of the ancient rhetoricians."— *Blair's Rhet.*, p. 122. "The putting letters together, so as to make words, is called spelling."—*Infant School Gram.*, p. 11. "What is the putting vowels and consonants together called?"—*Ib.*, p. 12. "Nobody knows of their being charitable but themselves."—*Fuller, on the Gospel*, p. 29. "Payment was at length made, but no reason assigned for its having been so long postponed."—*Murray's Gram.*, i, 186; *Kirkham's*, 194; *Ingersoll's*, 254. "Which will bear being brought into comparison with any composition of the kind."—*Blair's Rhet.*, p. 396. "To render vice ridiculous, is doing real service to the world."—*Ib.*,

p. 476. "It is copying directly from nature; giving a plain rehearsal of what passed, or was supposed to pass, in conversation."—*Ib.*, p. 433. "Propriety of pronunciation is giving to every word that sound, which the most polite usage of the language appropriates to it."—*Murray's Key*, 8vo, p. 200. "To occupy the mind, and prevent our regretting the insipidity of an uniform plain."—*Kames, El. of Crit.*, Vol. ii, p. 329. "There are a hundred ways of any thing happening."—*Steele.* "Tell me, signor, what was the cause of Antonio's sending Claudio to Venice, yesterday."—*Bucke's Gram.*, p 90. "Looking about for an outlet, some rich prospect unexpectedly opens to view."—*Kames, El. of Crit.*, ii, 334. "A hundred volumes of modern novels may be read, without acquiring a new idea"—*Webster's Essays*, p. 29. "Poetry admits of greater latitude than prose, with respect to coining, or, at least, new compounding words."—*Blair's Rhet.*, p. 93. "When laws were wrote on brazen tablets enforced by the sword."—*Notes to the Dunciad.* "A pronoun, which saves the naming a person or thing a second time, ought to be placed as near as possible to the name of that person or thing."—*Kames, El. of Crit.*, ii, 49. "The using a preposition in this case, is not always a matter of choice."—*Ib.*, ii, 37. "To save multiplying words, I would be understood to comprehend both circumstances."—*Ib.*, i, 219. "Immoderate grief is mute: complaining is struggling for consolation."—*Ib.*, i, 398. "On the other hand, the accelerating or retarding the natural course, excites a pain."—*Ib.*, i, 259. "Human affairs require the distributing our attention."—*Ib.*, i, 264. "By neglecting this circumstance, the following example is defective in neatness."—*Ib.*, ii, 29. "And therefore the suppressing copulatives must animate a description."—*Ib.*, ii, 32. "If the laying aside copulatives give force and liveliness, a redundancy of them must render the period languid."—*Ib.*, ii, 33. "It skills not asking my leave, said Richard."—*Scott's Crusaders.* "To redeem his credit, he proposed being sent once more to Sparta."—*Goldsmith's Greece*, i, 129. "Dumas relates his having given drink to a dog."—*Dr. Stone, on the Stomach*, p. 24. "Both are, in a like way, instruments of our receiving such ideas from external objects."—*Butler's Analogy*, p. 66. "In order to your proper handling such a subject."—*Spectator*, No. 533. "For I do not recollect its being preceded by an open vowel."—*Knight, on the Greek Alphabet*, p. 56. "Such is setting up the form above the power of godliness."—*Barclay's Works*, i, 72. "I remember walking once with my young acquaintance."— *Hunt's Byron*, p 27. "He [Lord Byron] did not like paying a debt."—*Ib.*, p. 74. "I do not remember seeing Coleridge when I was a child."—*Ib.*, p. 318. "In consequence of the dry rot's having been discovered, the mansion has undergone a thorough repair."—*Maunder's Gram.*, p. 17. "I would not advise the following entirely the German system."—DR. LIEBER: *Lit. Conv.*, p. 66. "Would it not be making the students judges of the professors?"—*Id., ib.*, p. 4. "Little time should intervene between their being proposed and decided upon."—PROF. VETHAKE: *ib.*, p. 39. "It would be nothing less than finding fault with the Creator."—*Ib.*, p. 116. "Having once been friends is a powerful reason, both of prudence and conscience, to restrain us from ever becoming enemies."—*Secker*. "By using the word as a conjunction, the ambiguity is prevented."—*Murray's Gram.*, i, 216.

"He forms his schemes the flood of vice to stem,
But preaching Jesus is not one of them."—*J. Taylor*.

LESSON VIII.—ADVERBS.

"Auxiliaries cannot only be inserted, but are really understood,"—*Wright's Gram.*, p 209. "He was since a hired Scribbler in the Daily Courant."—*Notes to the Dunciad*, ii, 299. "In gardening, luckily, relative beauty need never stand in opposition to intrinsic beauty."—*Kames, El. of Crit.*, ii, 330. "I doubt much of the propriety of the following examples."—*Lowth's Gram.*, p. 44. "And [we see] how far they have spread one of the worst

Languages possibly in this part of the world."—*Locke, on Ed.*, p. 341. "And in this manner to merely place him on a level with the beast of the forest."—*Smith's New Gram.*, p. 5. "Where, ah! where, has my darling fled?"—*Anon.* "As for this fellow, we know not from whence he is."—*John*, ix, 29. "Ye see then how that by works a man is justified, and not by faith only."—*James*, ii, 24. "The *Mixt* kind is where the poet speaks in his own person, and sometimes makes other characters to speak."—*Adam's Lat. Gram.*, p. 276; *Gould's*, 267. "Interrogation is, when the writer or orator raises questions and returns answers."—*Fisher's Gram.*, p. 154. "Prevention is, when an author starts an objection which he foresees may be made, and gives an answer to it."—*Ib.*, p. 154. "Will you let me alone, or no?"—*Walker's Particles*, p. 184. "Neither man nor woman cannot resist an engaging exterior."— *Chesterfield*, Let. lix. "Though the Cup be never so clean."—*Locke, on Ed.*, p. 65. "Seldom, or ever, did any one rise to eminence, by being a witty lawyer."—*Blair's Rhet.*, p. 272. "The second rule, which I give, respects the choice of subjects, from whence metaphors, and other figures, are to be drawn."—*Blair's Rhet.*, p. 144. "In the figures which it uses, it sets mirrors before us, where we may behold objects, a second time, in their likeness."—*Ib.*, p. 139. "Whose Business is to seek the true measures of Right and Wrong, and not the Arts how to avoid doing the one, and secure himself in doing the other."—*Locke, on Ed.*, p. 331. "The occasions when you ought to personify things, and when you ought not, cannot be stated in any precise rule."—*Cobbett's Eng. Gram.*, ¶ 182. "They reflect that they have been much diverted, but scarce can say about what."—*Kames, El. of Crit.*, i, 151. "The eyebrows and shoulders should seldom or ever be remarked by any perceptible motion."—*Adams's Rhet.*, ii, 389. "And the left hand or arm should seldom or never attempt any motion by itself."—*Ib.*, ii, 391. "Every speaker does not propose to please the imagination."—*Jamieson's Rhet.*, p. 104. "And like Gallio, they care little for none of these things."—*The Friend*, Vol. x, p. 351. "They may inadvertently be imitated, in cases where the meaning would be obscure."—*Murray's Gram.*, 8vo, p. 272. "Nor a man cannot make him laugh."—*Shak.* "The Athenians, in their present distress, scarce knew where to turn."—*Goldsmith's Greece*, i, 156. "I do not remember where ever God delivered his oracles by the multitude."—*Locke.* "The object of this government is twofold, outwards and inwards."—*Barclay's Works*, i, 553. "In order to rightly understand what we read."—*Johnson's Gram. Com.*, p. 313. "That a design had been formed, to forcibly abduct or kidnap Morgan."—*Stone, on Masonry*, p. 410. "But such imposture can never maintain its ground long."—*Blair's Rhet.*, p. 10. "But sure it is equally possible to apply the principles of reason and good sense to this art, as to any other that is cultivated among men."—*Ibid.* "It would have been better for you, to have remained illiterate, and to have been even hewers of wood."—*Murray's Gram.*, i, 374. "Dissyllables that have two vowels, which are separated in the pronunciation, have always the accent on the first syllable."—*Ib.*, i, 238. "And they all turned their backs without almost drawing a sword."—*Kames, El. of Crit.*, i, 224. "The principle of duty takes naturally place of every other."—*Ib.*, i, 342. "All that glitters is not gold."—*Maunder's Gram.*, p. 13. "Whether now or never so many myriads of ages hence."—*Pres. Edwards.*

"England never did, nor never shall,
Lie at the proud foot of a conqueror."—*Beaut. of Shak.*, p. 109.

LESSON IX.—CONJUNCTIONS.

"He readily comprehends the rules of Syntax, and their use and applicability in the examples before him."—*Greenleaf's Gram.*, p. 6. "The works of Æschylus have suffered more by time, than any of the ancient tragedians."—*Blair's Rhet.*, p. 470. "There is much more story, more bustle, and action, than on the French theatre."—*Ib.*, p. 478. "Such an unremitted anxiety and perpetual application as engrosses our whole time and thoughts, are forbidden."—SOAME JENYNS: *Tract*, p. 12. "It seems to be nothing else but the simple form of the adjective."—*Wright's Gram.*, p. 49. "But when I talk of *Reasoning*, I do not intend any other, but such as is suited to the Child's Capacity."—*Locke, on Ed.*, p. 129. "Pronouns have no other use in language, but to represent nouns."—*Jamieson's Rhet.*, p 83. "The speculative relied no farther on their own judgment, but to choose a leader, whom they implicitly followed."—*Kames, El. of Crit.*, Vol. i, p. xxv. "Unaccommodated man is no more but such a poor, bare, forked animal as thou art."—*Beaut. of Shak.*, p. 266. "A Parenthesis is a clause introduced into the body of a sentence obliquely, and which may be omitted without injuring the grammatical construction."—*Murray's Gram.*, i, 280; *Ingersoll's*, 292; *Smith's*, 192; *Alden's*, 162; *A. Flint's*, 114; *Fisk's*, 158; *Cooper's*, 187; *Comly's*, 163. "A Caret, marked thus ^ is placed where some word happens to be left *out in* writing, and which *is inserted over* the line."—*Murray's Gram.*, i, 282; *Ingersoll's*, 293; *and others*. "At the time that I visit them they shall be cast down."—*Jer.*, vi, 15. "Neither our virtues or vices are all our own."—DR. JOHNSON: *Sanborn's Gram.*, p. 167. "I could not give him an answer as early as he had desired."—*O. B. Peirce's Gram.*, p. 200. "He is not as tall as his brother."—*Nixon's Parser*, p. 124. "It is difficult to judge when Lord Byron is serious or not."—*Lady Blessington.* "Some nouns are both of the second and third declension."—*Gould's Lat. Gram.*, p. 48. "He was discouraged neither by danger or misfortune."—*Wells's Hist.*, p. 161. "This is consistent neither with logic nor history."—*The Dial*, i, 62. "Parts of Sentences are simple and compound."—*Blair's Gram.*, p. 114. "English verse is regulated rather by the number of syllables than of feet."—*Ib.*, p. 120. "I know not what more he can do, but pray for him."—*Locke, on Ed.*, p. 140. "Whilst they are learning, and apply themselves with Attention, they are to be kept in good Humour."—*Ib.*, p. 295. "A man cannot have too much of it, nor too perfectly."—*Ib.*, p. 322.

"That you may so run, as you may obtain; and so fight, as you may overcome."—*Wm. Penn.* "It is the case of some, to contrive false periods of business, because they may seem men of despatch."—*Lord Bacon.* "'A tall man and a woman.' In this sentence there is no ellipsis; the adjective or quality respect only the man."—*Dr. Ash's Gram.*, p. 95. "An abandonment of the policy is neither to be expected or desired."—*Pres. Jackson's Message*, 1830. "Which can be acquired by no other means but frequent exercise in speaking."—*Blair's Rhet.*, p. 344. "The chief and fundamental rules of syntax are common to the English as well as the Latin tongue."—*Ib.*, p. 90. "Then I exclaim, that my antagonist either is void of all taste, or that his taste is corrupted in a miserable degree."— *Ib.*, p. 21. "I cannot pity any one who is under no distress of body nor of mind."—*Kames, El. of Crit.*, i, 44. "There was much genius in the world, before there were learning or arts to refine it."—*Blair's Rhet.*, p. 391. "Such a Writer can have little else to do, but to new model the Paradoxes of ancient Scepticism."—*Brown's Estimate*, i, 102. "Our ideas of them being nothing else but a collection of the ordinary qualities observed in them."—*Duncan's Logic*, p. 25. "A *non-ens* or a negative can neither give pleasure nor pain."—*Kames, El. of Crit.*, i, 63. "So as they shall not justle and embarrass one another."—*Blair's Lectures*, p. 318. "He firmly refused to make use of any other voice but his own."— *Goldsmith's Greece*, i, 190. "Your marching regiments, Sir, will not make the guards their example, either as soldiers or subjects."—*Junius, Let.* 35. "Consequently, they had neither meaning, or beauty, to any but the natives of each country."—*Sheridan's Elocution*, p. 161.

"The man of worth, and has not left his peer,
Is in his narrow house for ever darkly laid."—*Burns.*

LESSON X.—PREPOSITIONS.

"These may be carried on progressively above any assignable limits."—*Kames, El. of Crit.*, i, 296. "To crowd in a single member of a period different subjects, is still worse than to crowd them into one period."—*Ib.*, ii, 27. "Nor do we rigidly insist for melodious prose."—*Ib.*, ii, 76. "The aversion we have at those who differ from us."—*Ib.*, ii, 365. "For we cannot bear his shifting the scene every line."—LD. HALIFAX: *ib.*, ii, 213. "We shall find that we come by it the same way."—*Locke.* "To this he has no better defense than that."—*Barnes's Bed Book*, p. 347. "Searching the person whom he suspects for having stolen his casket."—*Blair's Rhet.*, p. 479. "Who are elected as vacancies occur by the whole Board."—*Lit. Convention*, p. 81. "Almost the only field of ambition of a German, is science."—DR. LIEBER: *ib.*, p. 66. "The plan of education is very different to the one pursued in the sister country."—DR. COLEY, *ib.*, p. 197. "Some writers on grammar have contended that adjectives relate to, and modify the action of verbs."—*Wilcox's Gram.*, p. 61. "They are therefore of a mixed nature, participating of the properties both of pronouns and adjectives."—*Ingersoll's Gram.*, p. 57. "For there is no authority which can justify the inserting the aspirate or doubling the vowel."—*Knight, on Greek Alph.*, p. 52. "The distinction and arrangement between active, passive, and neuter verbs."—*Wright's Gram*, p. 176. "And see thou a hostile world *to* spread its delusive snares."—*Kirkham's Gram.*, p. 167. "He may be precaution'd, and be made see, how those joyn in the Contempt."—*Locke, on Ed.*, p. 155. "The contenting themselves now in the want of what they wish'd for, is a vertue."—*Ib.*, p. 185. "If the Complaint be of something really worthy your notice."—*Ib.*, p. 190. "True Fortitude I take to be the quiet Possession of a Man's self, and an undisturb'd doing his Duty."—*Ib.*, p. 204. "For the custom of tormenting and killing of Beasts will, by degrees, harden their Minds even towards Men."—*Ib.*, p. 216. "Children are whip'd to it, and made spend many Hours of their precious time uneasily in Latin."—*Ib.*, p. 289. "The ancient rhetoricians have entered into a very minute and particular detail of this subject; more particular, indeed, than any other that regards language."—*Jamieson's Rhet.*, p. 123. "But the one should not be omitted without the other."—*Bullions's Eng. Gram.*, p. 108. "In some of the common forms of speech, the relative pronoun is usually omitted."—*Murray's Gram.*, i, 218; *Weld's*, 191. "There are a great variety of causes, which disqualify a witness from being received to testify in particular cases."—*J. Q. Adams's Rhet.*, ii, 75. "Aside of all regard to interest, we should expect that," &c.—*Webster's Essays*, p. 82. "My opinion was given on a rather cursory perusal of the book."—*Murray's Key*, ii, 202. "And the next day, he was put on board his ship."—*Ib.*, ii, 201. "Having the command of no emotions but of what are raised by sight."—*Kames, El. of Crit.*, ii, 318. "Did these moral attributes exist in some other being beside himself."—*Wayland's Moral Science*, p. 161. "He did not behave in that manner out of pride or contempt of the tribunal."—*Goldsmith's Greece*, i, 190. "These prosecutions of William seem to have been the most iniquitous measures pursued by the court."—*Murray's Key*, 8vo, p. 199; *Priestley's Gram.*, 126. "To restore myself into the good graces of my fair critics."—*Dryden.* "Objects denominated beautiful, please not in virtue of any one quality common to them all."—*Blair's Rhet.*, p. 46. "This would have been less worthy notice, had not a writer or two of high rank lately adopted it."—*Churchill's Gram.*, p. 197.

"A Grecian youth, with talents rare,
Whom Plato's philosophic care," &c.—*Felton's Gram.*, p. 145.

LESSON XI.—PROMISCUOUS.

"To excel, is become a much less considerable object."—*Blair's Rhet.*, p. 351. "My robe, and my integrity to heaven, is all I now dare call mine own."—*Beauties of Shak.*, p. 173. "So thou the garland wear'st successively."—*Ib.*, p. 134. "For thou the garland wears successively."—*Enfield's Speaker*, p. 341. "If that thou need'st a Roman's, take it forth."—*Ib.*, p. 357. "If that thou be'st a Roman, take it forth."—*Beauties of Shak.*, p. 256. "If thou provest this to be real, thou must be a smart lad, indeed."—*Neef's Method of Teaching*, p. 210. "And another Bridge of four hundred Foot in Length."—*Brightland's Gram.*, p. 242. "*Metonomy* is putting one name for another on account of the near relation there is between them."—*Fisher's Gram.*, p. 151. "An *Antonomasia* is putting an appellative or common name for a proper name."—*Ib.*, p. 153. "Its being me needs make no difference in your determination."—*Bullions, E. Gram.*, p. 89. "The first and second page are torn."—*Ib.*, p. 145. "John's being from home occasioned the delay."—*Ib.*, p. 81. "His having neglected opportunities of improvement, was the cause of his disgrace."—*Ib.*, p. 81. "He will regret his having neglected opportunities of improvement when it may be too late."—*Ib.*, p. 81. "His being an expert dancer does not entitle him to our regard."—*Ib.*, p. 82.[443] "Cæsar went back to Rome to take possession of the public treasure, which his opponent, by a most unaccountable oversight, had neglected taking with him."—*Goldsmith's Rome*, p. 116. "And Cæsar took out of the treasury, to the amount of three thousand pound weight of gold, besides an immense quantity of silver."—*Ibid.* "Rules and definitions, which should always be clear and intelligible as possible, are thus rendered obscure."—*Greenleaf's Gram.*, p. 5. "So much both of ability and merit is seldom found."—*Murray's Key*, ii, 179. "If such maxims, and such practices prevail, what is become of decency and virtue?"—*Bullions, E. Gram.*, p. 78. "Especially if the subject require not so much pomp."—*Blair's Rhet.*, p. 117. "However, the proper mixture of light and shade, in such compositions; the exact adjustment of all the figurative circumstances with the literal sense; have ever been considered as points of great nicety."—*Murray's Gram.*, i, 343. "And adding to that hissing in our language, which is taken so much notice of by foreigners."—ADDISON:

DR. COOTE: *ib.*, i, 90. "Speaking impatiently to servants, or any thing that betrays unkindness or ill-humour, is certainly criminal."—*Murray's Key*, ii, 183; *Merchant's*, 190. "There is here a fulness and grandeur of expression well suited to the subject."—*Blair's Rhet.*, p. 218. "I single Strada out among the moderns, because he had the foolish presumption to censure Tacitus."—*Murray's Key*, ii, 262. "I single him out among the moderns, because," &c.—*Bolingbroke, on Hist.*, p. 116. "This is a rule not always observed, even by good writers, as strictly as it ought to be."—*Blair's Rhet.*, p. 103. "But this gravity and assurance, which is beyond boyhood, being neither wisdom nor knowledge, do never reach to manhood."—*Notes to the Dunciad.* "The regularity and polish even of a turnpike-road has some influence upon the low people in the neighbourhood."—*Kames, El. of Crit.*, ii, 358. "They become fond of regularity and neatness; which is displayed, first upon their yards and little enclosures, and next within doors."—*Ibid.* "The phrase, *it is impossible to exist*, gives us the idea of it's being impossible for men, or any body to exist."—*Priestley's Gram.*, p. 85. "I'll give a thousand pound to look upon him."—*Beauties of Shak.*, p. 151. "The reader's knowledge, as Dr. Campbell observes, may prevent his mistaking it."—*Murray's Gram.*, i, 172; *Crombie's*, 253. "When two words are set in contrast or in opposition to one another, they are both emphatic."—*Murray's Gram.*, i, 243. "The number of persons, men, women, and children, who were lost in the sea, was very great."—*Ib.*, ii, 20. "Nor is the resemblance between the primary and resembling object pointed out"—*Jamieson's Rhet.*, p. 179. "I think it the best book of the kind which I have met with."—DR. MATHEWS: *Greenleaf's Gram.*, p. 2.

"Why should not we their ancient rites restore,
And be what Rome or Athens were before."—*Roscommon*, p. 22.

LESSON XII.—TWO ERRORS.

"It is labour only which gives the relish to pleasure."—*Murray's Key*, ii, 234. "Groves are never as agreeable as in the opening of the spring."—*Ib.*, p. 216. "His 'Philosophical Inquiry into the origin of our Ideas on the Sublime and Beautiful' soon made him known to the literati."—*Biog. Rhet., n. Burke*. "An awful precipice or tower whence we look down on the objects which lie below."—*Blair's Rhet.*, p. 30. "This passage, though very poetical, is, however, harsh and obscure; owing to no other cause but this, that three distinct metaphors are crowded together."—*Ib.*, p. 149. "I propose making some observations."—*Ib.*, p. 280. "I shall follow the same method here which I have all along pursued."—*Ib.*, p. 346. "Mankind never resemble each other so much as they do in the beginnings of society."—*Ib.*, p. 380. "But no ear is sensible of the termination of each foot, in reading an hexameter line."—*Ib.*, p. 383. "The first thing, says he, which either a writer of fables, or of heroic poems, does, is, to choose some maxim or point of morality."—*Ib.*, p. 421. "The fourth book has been always most justly admired, and abounds with beauties of the highest kind."—*Ib.*, p. 439. "There is no attempt towards painting characters in the poem."—*Ib.*, p. 446. "But the artificial contrasting of characters, and the introducing them always in pairs, and by opposites, gives too theatrical and affected an air to the piece."—*Ib.*, p. 479. "Neither of them are arbitrary nor local."—*Kames, El. of Crit.*, p. xxi. "If crowding figures be bad, it is still worse to graft one figure upon another."—*Ib.*, ii, 236. "The crowding withal so many objects together, lessens the pleasure."—*Ib.*, ii, 324. "This therefore lies not in the putting off the Hat, nor making of Compliments."—*Locke, on Ed.*, p. 149. "But the Samaritan Vau may have been used, as the Jews did the Chaldaic, both for a vowel and consonant."—*Wilson's Essay*, p. 19. "But if a solemn and familiar pronunciation really exists in our language, is it not the business of a grammarian to mark both?"—*Walker's Dict., Pref.*, p. 4. "By making sounds follow each other agreeable to certain laws."—*Music of Nature*, p. 406. "If there was no drinking intoxicating draughts, there could be no drunkards."—*O. B. Peirce's Gram.*, p. 178. "Socrates knew his own defects, and if he was proud of any thing, it was in the being thought to have none."—*Goldsmith's Greece*, i, 188. "Lysander having brought his army to Ephesus, erected an arsenal for building of gallies."—*Ib.*, i, 161. "The use of these signs are worthy remark."—*Brightland's Gram.*, p. 94. "He received me in the same manner that I would you."—*Smith's New Gram.*, p. 113. "Consisting both of the direct and collateral evidence."—*Butler's Analogy*, p. 224. "If any man or woman that believeth have widows, let them relieve them, and let not the church be charged."—*1 Tim.*, v, 16. "For mens sakes are beasts bred."—*Walker's Particles*, p. 131. "From three a clock there was drinking and gaming."—*Ib.*, p. 141. "Is this he that I am seeking of, or no?"—*Ib.*, p. 248. "And for the upholding every one his own opinion, there is so much ado."—*Sewel's Hist.*, p. 809. "Some of them however will be necessarily taken notice of."—*Sale's Koran*, p. 71. "The boys conducted themselves exceedingly indiscreet."—*Merchant's Key*, p. 195. "Their example, their influence, their fortune, every talent they possess, dispense blessings on all around them."—*Ib.*, p. 197; *Murray's Key*, ii, 219. "The two *Reynolds* reciprocally converted one another"—*Johnson's Lives*, p. 185. "The destroying the two last Tacitus calls an attack upon virtue itself."—*Goldsmith's Rome*, p. 194. "Monies is your suit."—*Beauties of Shak.*, p. 38. "*Ch*, is commonly sounded like *tch*; as in church; but in words derived from the Greek, has the sound of *k*."—*Murray's Gram.*, i, 11. "When one is obliged to make some utensil supply purposes to which they were not originally destined."—*Campbell's Rhet.*, p. 222. "But that a being baptized with water, is a washing away of sin, thou canst not from hence prove."—*Barclay's Works*, i, 190. "Being but spoke to one, it infers no universal command."—*Ibid.* "For if the laying aside Copulatives gives Force and Liveliness, a Redundancy of them must render the Period languid."—*Buchanan's Syntax*, p. 134. "James used to compare him to a cat, who always fell upon her legs."—ADAM'S HIST. OF ENG.: *Crombie*, p. 384.

"From the low earth aspiring genius springs,
 And sails triumphant born on eagles wings."—*Lloyd*, p. 162.

LESSON XIII.—TWO ERRORS.

"An ostentatious, a feeble, a harsh, or an obscure style, for instance, are always faults."—*Blair's Rhet.* p. 190. "Yet in this we find the English pronounce perfectly agreeable to rule."—*Walker's Dict.*, p. 2. "But neither the perception of ideas, nor knowledge of any sort, are habits, though absolutely necessary to the forming of them."—*Butler's Analogy*, p. 111. "They were cast: and an heavy fine imposed upon them."—*Goldsmiths Greece*, ii, 30. "Without making this reflection, he cannot enter into the spirit, nor relish the composition of the author."—*Blair's Rhet.*, p. 450. "The scholar should be instructed relative to finding his words."—*Osborn's Key*, p. 4. "And therefore they could neither have forged, or reversified them."—*Knight, on the Greek Alph.*, p. 30. "A dispensary is the place where medicines are dispensed."—*Murray's Key*, ii, 172. "Both the connexion and number of words is determined by general laws."—*Neef's Sketch*, p. 73. "An Anapsest has the two first syllables unaccented, and the last accented: as, 'Contravene, acquiésce.'"—*Murray's Gram.*, i, 254. "An explicative sentence is, when a thing is said to be or not to be, to do or not to do, to suffer or not to suffer, in a direct manner."—*Ib.*, i, 141; *Lowth's*, 84. "BUT is a *conjunction*, in all cases when it is neither an adverb nor preposition."—*Smith's New Gram.*, p. 109. "He wrote in the king Ahasuerus' name, and sealed it with the king's ring."—*Esther*, viii, 10. "Camm and Audland were departed the town before this time."—*Sewel's Hist.*, p. 100. "Previous to their relinquishing the practice, they must be convinced."—*Dr. Webster, on Slavery*, p. 5. "Which he had thrown up previous to his setting out."—*Grimshaw's Hist. U. S.*, p. 84. "He left him to the value of an hundred drachmas in Persian money."—*Spect.*, No. 535. "All which the mind can ever contemplate concerning them, must be divided between the three."—*Cardell's Philad. Gram.*, p. 80. "Tom Puzzle is one of the most eminent immethodical disputants of any that has fallen under my observation."—*Spect.*, No. 476. "When you have once got him to think himself made amends for his suffering, by the praise is given him for his courage."—*Locke, on Ed*. §115. "In all matters where simple reason, and mere speculation is concerned."—*Sheridan's Elocution*, p. 136. "And therefore he should be spared the trouble of attending to any thing else, but his meaning."—*Ib.*, p. 105. "It is this kind of phraseology which is distinguished by the epithet *idiomatical*, and hath been originally the spawn, partly of ignorance, and partly of affectation."—*Campbell's Rhet.* p. 185. Murray has it—"and *which has* been originally," &c.—*Octavo Gram.* i, 370. "That neither the letters nor inflection are such as could have been employed by the ancient inhabitants of Latium."—*Knight, Gr. Alph.* p. 13, "In cases where the verb is intended to be applied to any one of the terms."—*Murray's Gram.,,* 150. "But this people which know not the law, are accursed."—*John*, vii, 49. "And the magnitude of the chorusses have weight and sublimity."—*Music of Nature*, p. 428. "Dare he deny but there are some of his fraternity guilty?"—*Barclays Works*, i, 327. "Giving an account of most, if not all the papers had passed betwixt them."—*Ib.*, i, 235. "In this manner, both as to parsing and correcting, all the rules of syntax should be treated, proceeding regularly according to their order."—*Murray's Exercises*, 12mo, p. x. "Ovando was allowed a brilliant retinue and a body guard."—*Sketch of Columbus*. "Is it I or he whom you requested to go?"—*Kirkham's Gram., Key*, p. 226. "Let thou and I go on."—*Bunyan's P. P.*, p. 158. "This I no-where affirmed; and do wholly deny."—*Barclay's Works*, iii, 454. "But that I deny; and remains for him to prove."—*Ibid.*

"Our country sinks beneath the yoke; It weeps, it bleeds, and each new day a gash Is added to her wounds."—SHAKSPEARE: *Joh. Dict., w. Beneath.* "Thou art the Lord who didst choose Abraham, and broughtest him forth out of Ur of the Chaldees."—*Murray's Key*, ii, 189. "He is the exhaustless fountain, from which emanates all these attributes, that exists throughout this wide creation."—*Wayland's Moral Science*, 1st Ed., p. 155. "I am he who have communed with the son of Neocles; I am he who have entered the gardens of pleasure."—*Wright's Athens*, p. 66.

"Such was in ancient times the tales received,
  Such by our good forefathers was believed."
    —*Rowe's Lucan*, B. ix, l. 605.

LESSON XIV.—TWO ERRORS.

"The noun or pronoun that stand before the active verb, may be called the agent."—*Alex. Murray's Gram.*, p. 121. "Such seems to be the musings of our hero of the grammar-quill, when he penned the first part of his grammar."—*Merchant's Criticisms.* "Two dots, the one placed above the other [:], is called Sheva, and represents a very short *e*."—*Wilson's Hebrew Gram.*, p. 43. "Great has been, and is, the obscurity and difficulty, in the nature and application of them."—*Butler's Analogy*, p. 184. "As two is to four, so is four to eight."—*Everest's Gram.*, p. 231. "The invention and use of it [arithmetic] reaches back to a period so remote as is beyond the knowledge of history."—*Robertson's America*, i, 288. "What it presents as objects of contemplation or enjoyment, fills and satisfies his mind."—*Ib.*, i, 377. "If he dare not say they are, as I know he dare not, how must I then distinguish?"—*Barclay's Works*, iii, 311. "He was now grown so fond of solitude that all company was become uneasy to him."—*Life of Cicero*, p. 32. "Violence and spoil is heard in her; before me continually is grief and wounds."—*Jeremiah*, vi, 7. "Bayle's Intelligence from the Republic of Letters, which make eleven volumes in duodecimo, are truly a model in this kind."—*Formey's Belles-Lettres*, p. 68. "To render pauses pleasing and expressive, they must not only be made in the right place, but also accompanied with a proper tone of voice."—*Murray's Gram.*, i, 249. "The opposing the opinions, and rectifying the mistakes of others, is what truth and sincerity sometimes require of us."—*Locke, on Ed.*, p. 211. "It is very probable that this assembly was called, to clear some doubt which the king had, about the lawfulness of the Hollanders' throwing off the monarchy of Spain, and withdrawing, entirely, their allegiance to that crown."—*Murray's Key*, ii, 195. "Naming the cases and numbers of a noun in their order is called declining it."—*Frost's El. of Gram.*, p. 10. "The embodying them is, therefore, only collecting such component parts of words."—*Town's Analysis*, p. 4. "The one is the voice heard at Christ's being baptized; the other, at his being transfigured."—*Barclays Works*, i, 267. "Understanding the literal sense would not have prevented their condemning the guiltless."—*Butler's Analogy*, p. 168. "As if this were taking the execution of justice out of the hand of God, and giving it to nature."—*Ib.*, p. 194. "They will say, you must conceal this good opinion of yourself; which yet is allowing the thing, though not the showing it."—*Sheffield's Works*, ii, 244. "So as to signify not only the doing an action, but the causing it to be done."—*Pike's Hebrew Lexicon*, p. 180. "This, certainly, was both dividing the unity of God, and limiting his immensity."—*Calvin's Institutes*, B. i, Ch. 13. "Tones being infinite in number, and varying in almost every individual, the arranging them under distinct heads, and reducing them to any fixed and permanent rules, may be considered as the last refinement in language."—*Knight, on Gr. Alph.*, p. 16. "The fierce anger of the Lord shall not return, until he have done it, and until he have performed the intents of his heart."—*Jeremiah*, xxx, 24. "We seek for more heroic and illustrious deeds, for more diversified and surprising events."—*Blair's Rhet.*, p. 373. "We distinguish the Genders, or the Male and Female Sex, four different Ways."—*Buchanan's Gram.*, p. 20. "Thus, ch and g, are ever hard. It is therefore proper to retain these sounds in Hebrew names, which have not been modernised, or changed by public use."—*Wilson's Essay on Gram.*, p. 24. "The Substantive or noun is the name of any thing conceived to subsist, or of which we have any notion."—*Lindley Murray's Gram.*, 2d Ed., p. 26. "The SUBSTANTIVE, or NOUN; being the name of any thing conceived to subsist, or of which we have any notion."—*Dr. Lowth's Gram.*, p. 6. "The *Noun* is the name of any thing that exists, or of which we have, or can form, an idea."—*Maunders Gram.*, p. 1. "A noun is the name of any thing in existence, or of which we can form an idea."—*Ib.*, p. 1. (See False Syntax under Note 7th to Rule 10th.) "The next thing to be taken Care of, is to keep him exactly to speaking of Truth."—*Locke, on Ed.*, p. 254. "The material, vegetable, and animal world, receive this influence according to their several capacities."—*The Dial*, i, 59. "And yet, it is fairly defensible on the principles of the schoolmen; if that can be called principles which consists merely in words."—*Campbell's Rhet.*, p. 274.

"Art thou so bare and full of wretchedness,
And fears to die? famine is in thy cheeks,
Need and oppression starveth in thy eyes."—*Beaut. of Shak.*, p. 317.

LESSON XV.—THREE ERRORS.

"The silver age is reckoned to have commenced on the death of Augustus, and continued to the end of Trajan's reign."—*Gould's Lat. Gram.*, p. 277. "Language is become, in modern times, more correct, indeed, and accurate."—*Blair's Rhet.*, p. 65. "It is evident, that words are most agreeable to the ear which are composed of smooth and liquid sounds, where there is a proper intermixture of vowels and consonants."—*Ib.*, p.

121. See *Murray's Gram.*, i, 325. "It would have had no other effect, but to add a word unnecessarily to the sentence."—*Blair's Rhet.*, p. 194. "But as rumours arose of the judges having been corrupted by money in this cause, these gave occasions to much popular clamour, and had thrown a heavy odium on Cluentius."—*Ib.*, p. 273. "A Participle is derived of a verb, and partakes of the nature both of the verb and the adjective."—*Dr. Ash's Gram.*, p. 39; *E. Devis's*, 9. "I will have learned my grammar before you learn your's."—*Wilbur and Liv. Gram.*, p. 14. "There is no earthly object capable of making such various and such forcible impressions upon the human mind as a complete speaker."—*Perry's Dict., Pref.* "It was not the carrying the bag which made Judas a thief and an hireling."—*South.* "As the reasonable soul and flesh is one man, so God and man is one Christ."—*Athanasian Creed.* "And I will say to them which were not my people, Thou art my people; and they shall say, Thou art my God."—*Hosea*, ii, 23. "Where there is nothing in the sense which requires the last sound to be elevated or emphatical, an easy fall, sufficient to show that the sense is finished, will be proper."—*Murray's Gram.*, i, 250. "Each party produces words where the letter *a* is sounded in the manner they contend for."—*Walker's Dict.*, p. 1. "To countenance persons who are guilty of bad actions, is scarcely one remove from actually committing them."—*Murray's Gram.*, i, 233. "'To countenance persons who are guilty of bad actions,' is part of a sentence, which is the nominative case to the verb 'is.'"—*Ibid.* "What is called splitting of particles, or separating a preposition from the noun which it governs, is always to be avoided."—*Blair's Rhet.*, p. 112; *Jamieson's*, 93. See *Murray's Gram.*, i, 319. "There is, properly, no more than one pause or rest in the sentence, falling betwixt the two members into which it is divided."—*Blair's Rhet.*, p. 125; *Jamieson's*, 126; *Murray's Gram.*, i, 329. "Going barefoot does not at all help on the way to heaven."—*Steele, Spect.*, No. 497. "There is no Body but condemns this in others, though they overlook it in themselves."—*Locke, on Ed.*, §145. "In the same sentence, be

careful not to use the same word too frequently, nor in different senses."—*Murray's Gram.*, i, 296. "Nothing could have made her so unhappy, as marrying a man who possessed such principles."—*Murray's Key*, ii, 200. "A warlike, various, and a tragical age is best to write of, but worst to write in."—*Cowley's Pref.*, p. vi. "When thou instances Peter his baptizing Cornelius."—*Barclay's Works*, i, 188. "To introduce two or more leading thoughts or agents, which have no natural relation to, or dependence on one another."—*Murray's Gram.*, i, 313. "Animals, again, are fitted to one another, and to the elements where they live, and to which they are as appendices."—*Ibid.* "This melody, or varying the sound of each word so often, is a proof of nothing, however, but of the fine ear of that people."—*Jamieson's Rhet.*, p. 5. "They can each in their turns be made use of upon occasion."—*Duncan's Logic*, p. 191. "In this reign lived the poet Chaucer, who, with Gower, are the first authors who can properly be said to have written English."—*Bucke's Gram.*, p. 144. "In the translating these kind of expressions, consider the IT IS, as if it were *they*, or *they are*."—*Walker's Particles*, p. 179. "The chin has an important office to perform; for upon its activity we either disclose a polite or vulgar pronunciation."—*Music of Nature*, p. 27. "For no other reason, but his being found in bad company."—*Webster's Amer. Spelling-Book*, p. 96. "It is usual to compare them in the same manner as Polisyllables."—*Priestley's Gram.*, p. 77. "The infinitive mood is recognised easier than any others, because the preposition *to* precedes it."—*Bucke's Gram.*, p, 95. "Prepositions, you recollect, connect words as well as conjunctions: how, then, can you tell the one from the other?"—*Smith's New Gram.*, p. 38.

"No kind of work requires so nice a touch,
And if well finish'd, nothing shines so much"
    —*Sheffield, Duke of Buck.*

LESSON XVI—THREE ERRORS.

"It is the final pause which alone, on many occasions, marks the difference between prose and verse; which will be evident from the following arrangement of a few poetical lines."—*Murray's Gram.*, i, 260. "I shall do all I can to persuade others to take the same measures for their cure which I have."—GUARDIAN: see *Campbell's Rhet.*, p. 207. "I shall do all I can, to persuade others to take the same measures for their cure which I have taken."—*Murray's Key*, ii, 215. "It is the nature of extreme self-lovers, as they will set an house on fire, and [or *an*] it were but to roast their eggs."—*Ld. Bacon.* "Did ever man struggle more earnestly in a cause where both his honour and life are concerned?"—*Duncan's Cicero*, p. 15. "So the rests and pauses, between sentences and their parts, are marked by points."—*Lowth's Gram.*, p. 114. "Yet the case and mode is not influenced by them, but determined by the nature of the sentence."—*Ib.*, p. 113. "By not attending to this rule, many errors have been committed: a number of which is subjoined, as a further caution and direction to the learner."—*Murray's Gram.*, i, 114. "Though thou clothest thyself with crimson, though thou deckest thee with ornaments of gold, though thou rentest thy face with painting, in vain shalt thou make thyself fair."—*Jeremiah*, iv, 30. "But that the doing good to others will make us happy, is not so evident; feeding the hungry, for example, or clothing the naked."—*Kames, El. of Crit.*, i, 161. "There is no other God but him, no other light but his."—*William Penn.* "How little reason to wonder, that a perfect and accomplished orator, should be one of the characters that is most rarely found?"—*Blair's Rhet.*, p. 337. "Because they neither express doing nor receiving an action."—*Infant School Gram.*, p. 53. "To find the answers, will require an effort of mind, and when given, will be the result of reflection, showing that the subject is understood."—*Ib.*, p. vii. "To say, that 'the sun rises,' is trite and common; but it becomes a magnificent image when expressed as Mr. Thomson has done."—*Blair's Rhet.*, p. 137. "The declining a word is the giving it different endings."—*Ware's Gram.*, p. 7. "And so much are they for every one's following their own mind."—*Barclay's Works*, i, 462. "More than one overture for a peace was made, but Cleon prevented their taking effect."—*Goldsmith's Greece*, i, 121. "Neither in English or in any other language is this word, and that which corresponds to it in other languages, any more an article, than *two, three, four*."—DR. WEBSTER: *Knickerbocker of 1836*. "But the most irksome conversation of all others I have met within the neighbourhood, has been among two or three of your travellers."—*Spect.*, No. 474. "Set down the two first terms of supposition under each other in the first place."—*Smiley's Arithmetic*, p. 79. "It is an useful rule too, to fix our eye on some of the most distant persons in the assembly."—*Blair's Rhet.*, p. 328. "He will generally please most, when pleasing is not his sole nor chief aim."—*Ib.*, p. 336. "At length, the consuls return to the camp, and inform them they could receive no other terms but that of surrendering their arms, and passing under the yoke."—*Ib.*, p. 360. "Nor is mankind so much to blame, in his choice thus determining him."—SWIFT: *Crombie's Treatise*, p 360. "These forms are what is called Number."—*Fosdick's De Sacy*, p. 62. "In languages which admit but two Genders, all Nouns are either Masculine or Feminine, even though they designate beings which are neither male or female."—*Ib.*, p. 66. "It is called a *Verb* or *Word* by way of eminence, because it is the most essential word in a sentence, without which the other parts of speech can form no complete sense."—*Gould's Adam's Gram.*, p. 76. "The sentence will consist of two members, which are commonly separated from one another by a comma."—*Jamieson's Rhet.*, p. 7. "Loud and soft in speaking, is like the *fortè* and *piano* in music, it only refers to the different degrees of force used in the same key; whereas high and low imply a change of key."—*Sheridan's Elocution*, p. 116. "They are chiefly three: the acquisition of knowledge; the assisting the memory to treasure up this knowledge; or the communicating it to others."—*Ib.*, p. 11.

"These kind of knaves I know, which in this plainness,
  Harbour more craft, and more corrupter ends,
  Than twenty silly ducking observants."—*Beauties of Shak.*, p. 261.

LESSON XVII.—MANY ERRORS.

"A man will be forgiven, even great errors, in a foreign language; but in his own, even the least slips are justly laid hold of, and ridiculed."—*American Chesterfield*, p 83. "*Let* does not only express permission; but praying, exhorting, commanding."—*Lowth's Gram.*, p. 41. "*Let*, not only expresses permission, but entreating, exhorting, commanding."—*Murray's Gram.*, p. 88; *Ingersoll's*, 135. "That death which is our leaving this world, is nothing else but putting off these bodies."—*Sherlock*. "They differ from the saints recorded both in the Old and New Testaments."—*Newton*. "The nature therefore of relation consists in the referring or comparing two things one to another; from which comparison, one or both comes to be denominated"—*Locke's Essay*, i, 220. "It is not credible, that there hath been any one who through the whole course of their lives will say, that they have kept themselves undefiled with the least spot or stain of sin."—*Witsius*. "If acting conformably to the will of our Creator;—if promoting the welfare of mankind around us;—if securing our own happiness;—are objects of the highest moment:—then we are loudly called upon to cultivate and extend the great interests of religion and virtue"—*Murray's Gram.*, i, 278; *Comly's*, 163; *Ingersoll's*, 291. "By the verb being in the plural number, it is supposed that it has a plural nominative, which is not the case. The only nominative to the verb, is, *the officer*: the expression *his guard*, are in the objective case, governed by the preposition *with*; and they cannot consequently form the nominative, or any part of it. The prominent subject, and the true nominative of the verb, and to which the verb peculiarly refers, is *the officer*."—*Murray's Parsing*, Cr. 8vo, ii, 22. "This is another use, that, in my opinion, contributes rather to make a man learned than wise; and is neither capable of pleasing the understanding, or imagination."—ADDISON: *Churchill's Gram.*, p. 353. "The work is a dull performance; and is capable of pleasing neither the understanding, nor the imagination."—*Murray's Key*, ii, 210. "I would recommend the Elements of English Grammar, by Mr. Frost. Its plan is after Murray, but his definitions and language is simplified as far as the nature of the subject will admit, to meet the understanding of children. It also embraces more copious examples and exercises in Parsing than is usual in elementary treatises."—*Hall's Lectures on School-Keeping*, 1st Ed., p. 37. "More rain falls in the first two summer months, than in the first two winter ones: but it makes a much greater show upon the earth, in these than in those; because there is a much slower evaporation."—*Murray's Key*, ii, 189. See *Priestley's Gram.*, p. 90. "They often contribute also to the rendering some persons prosperous though wicked: and, which is still worse, to the rewarding some actions though vicious, and punishing other actions though virtuous."—*Butler's Analogy*, p. 92. "From hence, to such a man, arises naturally a secret satisfaction and sense of security, and implicit hope of somewhat further."—*Ib.*, p. 93. "So much for the third and last cause of illusion that was taken notice of, arising from the abuse of very general and abstract terms, which is the principal source of all the nonsense that hath been vented by metaphysicians, mystagogues, and theologians."—*Campbell's Rhet.*, p. 297. "As to those animals whose use is less common, or who on account of the places which they inhabit, fall less under our observation, as fishes and birds, or whom their diminutive size removes still further from our observation, we generally, in English, employ a single Noun to designate both Genders, Masculine and Feminine."—*Fosdick's De Sacy*, p. 67. "Adjectives may always be distinguished by their being the word, or words, made use of to describe the quality, or condition, of whatever is mentioned."—*Emmons's Gram.*, p. 20. "Adverb signifies a word added to a verb, participle, adjective, or other adverb, to describe or qualify their qualities."—*Ib.*, p. 64. "The joining together two such grand objects, and the representing them both as subject, at one moment, to the command of God, produces a noble effect."—*Blair's Rhet.*, p. 37. "Twisted columns, for instance, are undoubtedly ornamental; but as they have an appearance of weakness, they always displease when they are made use of to support any part of a building that is massy, and that seems to require a more substantial prop."—*Ib.*, p. 40. "Upon a vast number of inscriptions, some upon rocks, some upon stones of a defined shape, is found an Alphabet different from the Greeks, Latins, and Hebrews, and also unlike that of any modern nation."—*Fowler's E. Gram.*, 8vo, 1850, p. 176.

LESSON XVIII—MANY ERRORS.

"'The empire of Blefuscu is an island situated to the northeast side of Lilliput, from whence it is parted only by a channel of 800 yards wide.' *Gulliver's Travels*. The ambiguity may be removed thus:—'from whence it is parted by a channel of 800 yards wide only.'"—*Kames, El. of Crit.*, ii, 44. "The nominative case is usually the agent or doer, and always the subject of the verb."—*Smith's New Gram.*, p. 47. "There is an originality, richness, and variety in his [Spenser's] allegorical personages, which almost vies with the splendor of the ancient mythology."—*Hazlitt's Lect.*, p. 68. "As neither the Jewish nor Christian revelation have been universal, and as they have been afforded to a greater or less part of the world at different times; so likewise, at different times, both revelations have had different degrees of evidence."—*Butler's Analogy*, p. 210. "Thus we see, that killing a man with a sword or a hatchet, are looked upon as no distinct species of action: but if the point of the sword first enter the body, it passes for a distinct species, called *stabbing*."—*Locke's Essay*, p. 314. "If a soul sin, and commit a trespass against the Lord, and lie unto his neighbour in that which was delivered him to keep, or hath deceived his neighbour, or have found that which was lost, and lieth concerning it, and sweareth falsely; in any of all these that a man doeth, sinning therein, then it shall be," &c.—*Lev.*, vi, 2. "As the doing and teaching the commandments of God is the great proof of virtue, so the breaking them, and the teaching others to break them, is the great proof of vice."—*Wayland's Moral Science,* p. 281. "In Pope's terrific maltreatment of the latter simile, it is neither true to mind or eye."—*Coleridge's Introd.,* p. 14. "And the two brothers were seen, transported with rage and fury, endeavouring like Eteocles and Polynices to plunge their swords into each other's hearts, and to assure themselves of the throne by the death of their rival."—*Goldsmith's Greece,* i, 176. "Is it not plain, therefore, that neither the castle, the planet, nor the cloud, which you see here, are those real ones, which you suppose exist at a distance?"—*Berkley's Alciphron,* p 166. "I have often wondered how it comes to pass, that every Body should love themselves best, and yet value their neighbours Opinion about themselves more than their own."—*Collier's Antoninus,* p. 226. "VIRTUE ([Greek: Aretahe], Virtus) as well as most of its Species, are all Feminine, perhaps from their Beauty and amiable appearance."—*Harris's Hermes,* p. 55. "Virtue, with most of its Species, are all Feminine, from their Beauty and amiable Appearance; and so Vice becomes Feminine of Course, as being Virtue's natural opposite."—*British Gram.,* p. 97. "Virtue, with most of its Species, is Feminine, and so is Vice, for being Virtue's opposite."—*Buchanan's Gram.,* p. 22. "From this deduction, may be easily seen how it comes to pass, that personification makes so great a figure in all compositions, where imagination or passion have any concern."—*Blair's Rhet.,* p. 155. "An Article is a word prefixed to a substantive to point them out, and to show how far their signification extends."—*Folker's Gram.,* p. 4. "All men have certain natural, essential, and inherent rights—among which are, the enjoying and defending life and liberty; acquiring, possessing, and protecting property; and, in a word, of seeking and obtaining happiness."—*Constitution of New Hampshire.* "From Grammarians who form their ideas, and make their decisions, respecting this part of English Grammar, on the principles and construction of languages, which, in these points, do not suit the peculiar nature of our own, but differ considerably from it, we may naturally expect grammatical schemes that are not very perspicuous, or perfectly consistent, and which will tend more to perplex than inform the learner."—*Murray's Gram.*, p. 68; *Hall's*, 15. "There are, indeed, very few who know how to be idle and innocent, or have a relish of any pleasures that are not criminal; every diversion they take, is at the expense of some one virtue or another, and their very first step out of business is into vice or folly."—ADDISON: *Blair's Rhet.*, p. 201.[444]

"Hail, holy love! thou word that sums all bliss!
Gives and receives all bliss: fullest when most
Thou givest; spring-head of all felicity!"
—*Pollok, C. of T.*, B. v, 1, 193.

GENERAL RULE.

The following comprehensive canon for the correction of all sorts of nondescript errors in syntax, and the several critical or general notes under it, seem necessary for the completion of my design; which is, to furnish a thorough exposition of the various faults against which the student of English grammar has occasion to be put upon his guard.

GENERAL RULE OF SYNTAX.

In the formation of sentences, the consistency and adaptation of all the words should be carefully observed; and a regular, clear, and correspondent construction should be preserved throughout.

CRITICAL NOTES TO THE GENERAL RULE.

CRITICAL NOTE I.—OF THE PARTS OF SPEECH.

Words that may constitute different parts of speech, must not be left doubtful as to their classification, or to what part of speech they belong.

CRITICAL NOTE II.—OF DOUBTFUL REFERENCE.

The reference of words to other words, or their syntactical relation according to the sense, should never be left doubtful, by any one who means to be understood.

CRITICAL NOTE III.—OF DEFINITIONS.

A definition, in order to be perfect, must include the whole thing, or class of things, which it pretends to define, and exclude every thing which comes not under the name.

CRITICAL NOTE IV.—OF COMPARISONS.

A comparison is a form of speech which requires some similarity or common property in the things compared; without which, it becomes a solecism.

CRITICAL NOTE V.—OF FALSITIES.

Sentences that convey a meaning manifestly false, should be changed, rejected, or contradicted; because they distort language from its chief end, or only worthy use; which is, to state facts, and to tell the truth. CRITICAL NOTE VI.—OF ABSURDITIES.

Absurdities, of every kind, are contrary to grammar, because they are contrary to reason, or good sense, which is the foundation of grammar.

CRITICAL NOTE VII.—OF SELF-CONTRADICTION.

Every writer or speaker should be careful not to contradict himself; for what is self-contradictory, is both null in argument, and bad in style.

CRITICAL NOTE VIII.—OF SENSELESS JUMBLING.

To jumble together words without care for the sense, is an unpardonable negligence, and an abuse of the human understanding.

CRITICAL NOTE IX.—OF WORDS NEEDLESS.

Words that are entirely needless, and especially such as injure or encumber the expression, ought in general to be omitted.

CRITICAL NOTE X.—OF IMPROPER OMISSIONS.

Words necessary to the sense, or even to the melody or beauty of a sentence, ought seldom, if ever, to be omitted.

CRITICAL NOTE XI.—OF LITERARY BLUNDERS.

Grave blunders made in the name of learning, are the strongest of all certificates against the books which contain them unreproved.

CRITICAL NOTE XII.—OF PERVERSIONS.

Proof-texts in grammar, if not in all argument, should be quoted literally; and even that which needs to be corrected, must never be perverted.

CRITICAL NOTE XIII.—OF AWKWARDNESS.

Awkwardness, or inelegance of expression, is a reprehensible defect in style, whether it violate any of the common rules of syntax or not.

CRITICAL NOTE XIV.—OF IGNORANCE.

Any use of words that implies ignorance of their meaning, or of their proper orthography, is particularly unscholarlike; and, in proportion to the author's pretensions to learning, disgraceful.

CRITICAL NOTE XV.—OF SILLINESS. Silly remarks and idle truisms are traits of a feeble style, and, when their weakness is positive, or inherent, they ought to be entirely omitted. CRITICAL NOTE XVI.—OF THE INCORRIGIBLE.

Passages too erroneous for correction, may be criticised, orally or otherwise, and then passed over without any attempt to amend them.[445]

GENERAL OBSERVATIONS ON THE SYNTAX.

OBS. 1.—In the foregoing code of syntax, the author has taken the parts of speech in their order, and comprised all the general principles of relation, agreement, and government, in twenty-four leading Rules. Of these rules, eight—(namely, the 1st, of *Articles*; the 4th, of *Possessives*; the 9th, of *Adjectives*; the 20th, of *Participles*; the 21st, of *Adverbs*; the 22d, of *Conjunctions*; the 23d, of *Prepositions*; and the 24th, of *Interjections*—) are used only in parsing. The remaining sixteen, because they embrace principles that are sometimes violated in practice, answer the double purpose of parsing and correcting. The Exceptions, of which there are thirty-two, (all occasionally applicable in parsing,) belong to nine different rules, and refer to all the parts of speech, except nouns and interjections. The Notes, of which there are one hundred and fifty-two, are subordinate rules of syntax, not designed to be used in parsing, but formed for the exposition and correction of so many different forms of false grammar. The Observations, of which there are, in this part of the work, without the present series, four hundred and ninety-seven, are designed not only to defend and confirm the doctrines adopted by the author, but to explain the arrangement of words, and whatever is difficult or peculiar in construction.

OBS. 2.—The rules in a system of syntax may be more or less comprehensive, as well as more or less simple or complex; consequently they may, without deficiency or redundance, be more or less numerous. But either complexity or vagueness, as well as redundance or deficiency, is a fault; and, when all these faults are properly avoided, and the two great ends of methodical syntax, *parsing* and *correcting*, are duly answered, perhaps the requisite number of syntactical rules, or grammatical canons, will no longer appear very indeterminate. In the preceding chapters, the essential principles of English syntax are supposed to be pretty fully developed; but there are yet to be exhibited some forms of error, which must be corrected under other heads or maxims, and for the treatment of which the several dogmas of this chapter are added. Completeness in the system, however, does not imply that it must have shown the pupil how to correct every form of language that is amiss: for there may be in composition many errors of such a nature that no rule of grammar can show, either what should be substituted for the faulty expression, or what fashion of amendment may be the most eligible. The inaccuracy may be gross and obvious, but the correction difficult or impossible. Because the sentence may require a change throughout; and a total change is not properly a correction; it is a substitution of something new, for what was, perhaps, in itself incorrigible.

OBS. 3.—The notes which are above denominated *Critical* or *General*, are not all of them obviously different in kind from the other notes; but they all are such as could not well have been placed in any of the earlier chapters of the book. The *General Rule of Syntax*, since it is not a canon to be used in parsing, but one that is to be applied only in the correcting of false syntax, might seem perhaps to belong rather to this order of notes; but I have chosen to treat it with some peculiar distinction, because it is not only more comprehensive than any other rule or note, but is in one respect more important; it is the rule which will be cited for the correction of the greatest number and variety of errors. Being designed to meet every possible form of inaccuracy in the mere construction of sentences,—or, at least, every corrigible solecism by which any principle of syntax can be violated,—it necessarily includes almost all the other rules and notes. It is too broad to convey very definite instruction, and therefore ought not in general to be applied where a more particular rule or note is clearly applicable. A few examples, not properly fitting under any other head, will serve to show its use and application: such examples are given, in great abundance, in the false syntax below. If, in some of the instances selected, this rule is applied to faults that might as well have been corrected by some other, the choice, in such cases, is deemed of little or no importance.

OBS. 4.—The imperfection of *ancient* writing, especially in regard to division and punctuation, has left the syntactical relation of words, and also the sense of passages, in no few instances, uncertain; and has consequently made, where the text has been thought worthy of it, an abundance of difficult work for translators, critics, and commentators. Rules of grammar, now made and observed, as they ought to be, may free the compositions of this, or a future age, from similar embarrassments; and it is both just and useful, to test our authors by them, criticising or correcting their known blunders according to the present rules of accurate writing. But the readers and expounders of what has come to us from remote time, can be rightly guided only by such principles and facts as have the stamp of creditable antiquity. Hence there are, undoubtedly, in books, some errors and defects which have outlived the *time in which*, and the *authority b which*, they might have been corrected. As we have no right to make a man say that which he himself never said or intended to say, so we have in fact none to fix a positive meaning upon his language, without knowing for a certainty what he meant by it. Reason, or good sense, which, as I have suggested, is the foundation of grammar and of all good writing, is indeed a perpetual as well as a universal principle; but, since the exercises of our reason must, from the very nature of the faculty, be limited to what we know and understand, we are not competent to the positive correction, or to the sure translation, of what is obscure and disputable in the standard books of antiquity.

OBS. 5.—Let me cite an example: "For all this I considered in my heart, even to declare all this, that the righteous, and the wise, and their works, are in the hand of God: no man knoweth either love or hatred *by* all *that is* before them. All *things come* alike to all."— *Ecclesiastes,* ix, 1. Here is, doubtless, *one* error which any English scholar may point out or correct. The pronoun "*them*" should be *him,* because its intended antecedent appears to be "*man,*" and not "*the righteous and the wise,*" going before. But are there not *other* faults in the version? The common French Bible, in this place, has the following import: "Surely I have applied my heart to all that, and to unfold all this; *to wit,* that the righteous and the wise, and their actions, *are* in the hand of God and love and hatred; *and that* men know nothing of all *that which is* before them. All *happens* equally to all." The Latin Vulgate gives this sense: "All these things have I considered in my heart, that I might understand them accurately: the righteous and the wise, and their works, are in the hand of God; and yet man doth not know, whether by love or by hatred lie may be worthy: but all things in the future are kept uncertain, so that all may happen alike to the righteous man and to the wicked." In the Greek of the Septuagint, the introductory members of this passage are left at the end of the preceding chapter, and are literally thus: "that all this I received into my heart, and my heart understood all this." The rest, commencing a new chapter, is as follows: "For the righteous and the wise and their works *are* in the hand of God, and indeed both love and hatred man knoweth not: all things before their face *are* vanity to all." Now, which of these several readings is the nearest to what Solomon meant by the original text, or which is the farthest from it, and therefore the most faulty, I leave it to men more learned than myself to decide; but, certainly, there is no *inspired authority* in any of them, but *in so far as they convey the sense which he really intended.* And if his meaning had not been, by some imperfection in the oldest expression we have of it, *obscured and partly lost,* there could be neither cause nor excuse for these discrepancies. I say this with no willingness to depreciate the general authority of the Holy Scriptures, which are for the most part clear in their import, and very ably translated into English, as well as into other languages.

IMPROPRIETIES FOR CORRECTION.

FALSE SYNTAX UNDER THE GENERAL RULE.

LESSON I.—ARTICLES.

(1.) "An article is a part of speech placed before nouns."—*Comly's Gram.*, p. 11.

[FORMULE.—Not proper, because the article *an* is here inconsistent with the term "*part of speech*;" for the text declares one thing of a kind to be the whole kind. But, according to the General Rule of Syntax, "In the formation of sentences, the consistency and adaptation of all the words should be carefully observed; and a regular, clear, and correspondent construction should be preserved throughout." The sentence may be corrected in two ways, thus: "*The* article is a part of speech placed before nouns;"—or better, "*An* article is a word placed before nouns." [446]]

(2.) "An article is a part of speech used to limit nouns."—*Gilbert's Gram.*, p. 19. (3.) "An article is a part of speech set before nouns to fix their vague Signification."—*Ash's Gram.*, p. 18. (4.) "An adjective is a part of speech used to describe a noun."—*Gilbert's Gram.*, p. 19. (5.) "A pronoun is a part of speech used instead of a noun."—*Ibid.*; and *Weld's Gram.*, pp. 30 and 50; *Abridg.*, pp. 29 and 46. (6.) "A Pronoun is a Part of Speech which is often used instead of a Noun Substantive common, and supplies the Want of a Noun proper."—*British Gram.*, p. 102; *Buchanan's Gram.*, p. 29. (7.) "A verb is a part of speech, which signifies *to be, to do, or to be acted upon*"—*Merchant's School Gram.*, p. 17. (8.) "A verb is a part of speech, which signifies *to be, to act, or to receive an action.*"—*Comly's Gram.*, p. 11. (9.) "A verb is a part of speech by which any thing is asserted."—*Weld's Gram*, p. 50; *Abridg.*, 46 and 58. (10.) "A verb is a part of speech which expresses action, or existence, in a direct manner."—*Gilbert's Gram.*, p. 20. (11.) "A participle is a part of speech derived from a verb, and expresses action or existence in an indirect manner."—*Ibid.* (12.) "A Participle is a Part of Speech derived from a Verb, and denotes being, doing, or suffering, and implies Time, as a Verb does."—*British Gram.*, p. 139; *Buchanan's*, p. 46. "An adverb is a part of speech used to add to the meaning of verbs, adjectives, and participles."—*Gilbert's Gram.*, p. 20. (14.) "An adverb is an indeclinable part of speech, added to a verb, adjective, or other adverb, to express some circumstance, quality, or manner of their signification."— *Adam's Gram.*, p. 142; *Gould's*, 147. (15.) "An Adverb is a part of speech joined to a verb, an Adjective, a Participle, and sometimes to another Adverb, to express the quality or circumstance of it."—*Ash's Gram.*, p. 47, (16.) "An Adverb is a part of speech joined to a Verb, Adjective, Participle, and sometimes to another Adverb, to express some circumstances respecting it."—*Beck's Gram.*, p. 23. (17.) "An Adverb is a Part of Speech which is joined to a Verb, Adjective, Participle, or to another Adverb to express some Modification, or Circumstance, Quality, or

Manner of their Signification."—*Buchanan's Gram.*, p. 61. (18.) "An Adverb is a part of speech added to a Verb (whence the name), and sometimes even to another word."—*Bucke's Gram.*, p. 76. (19.) "A conjunction is a part of speech used to connect words and sentences."—*Gilbert's Gram.*, p. 20; *Weld's*, 51. (20.) "A Conjunction is a part of speech that joins words or sentences together."—*Ash's Gram.*, p. 43. (21.) "A Conjunction is that part of speech which connect sentences, or parts of sentences or single words."—*Blair's Gram.*, p. 41. (22.) "A Conjunction is a part of speech, that is used principally to connect sentences, so as, out of two, three, or more, sentences, to make one."—*Bucke's Gram.*, p. 28. (23.) "A Conjunction is a part of speech that is chiefly used to connect sentences, joining two or more simple sentences into one compound sentence: it sometimes connects only words."—*Kirkham's Gram.*, p. 118. (24.) "A Conjunction is a Part of Speech which joins Sentences together, and shews the Manner of their Dependance upon one another."—*British Gram.*, p. 163; *Buchanan's*, p. 64; *E. Devis's*. 103. (25.) "A preposition is a part of Speech used to show the relation between other words."—*Gilbert's Gram.*, p. 20. (26.) "A Preposition is a part of speech which serves to connect words and show the relation between them."—*Frost's El. of Gram.*, p. 42. (27.) "A *preposition* is a part of speech used to connect words and show their relation."—*Weld's Gram.*, p. 51; *Abridg.* 47. (28.) "A preposition is that part of speech which shows the position of persons or things, or the relation that one noun or pronoun bears toward another."—*Blair's Gram.*, p. 40. (29.) "A Preposition is a Part of Speech, which being added to any other Parts of Speech serves to shew their State, Relation or Reference to each other."—*British Gram.*, p. 165; *Buchanan's*, p. 65. (30.) "An interjection is a part of speech used to express sudden passion or emotion."—*Gilbert's Gram.*, p. 20. (31.) "An interjection is a part of speech used in giving utterance to some sudden feeling or emotion."— *Weld's Gram.*, pp. 49 and 51; *Abridg.*, 44 and 47. (32.) "An Interjection is that part of speech which denotes any sudden affection or emotion of the mind."—*Blair's Gram.*, p. 42. (33) "An Interjection is a Part of Speech thrown into discourse, and denotes some sudden Passion or Emotion of the Soul."—*British Gram.*, p. 172; *Buchanan's*, p. 67.

(34.) "A scene might tempt some peaceful sage
To rear him a lone hermitage."
—*Union Poems*, p. 89.

(35.) "Not all the storms that shake the pole
Can e'er disturb thy halcyon soul,
And smooth th' unaltered brow."
—*Day's Gram.*, p. 78; *E. Reader*, 230.

LESSON II.—NOUNS. "The thrones of every monarchy felt the shock."—*Frelinghuysen.*

[FORMULE.—Not proper, because the plural noun *thrones* has not a clear and regular construction, adapted to the author's meaning. But, according to the General Rule of Syntax, "In the formation of sentences the consistency and adaptation of all the words should be carefully observed; and a regular, clear, and correspondent construction should be preserved throughout." The sentence may be corrected thus: "The *throne* of every monarchy felt the shock."]

"These principles ought to be deeply impressed upon the minds of every American."—*Webster's Essays*, p. 44. "The word *church* and *shire* are radically the same."—*Ib.*, p. 256. "They may not, in their present form, be readily accommodated to every circumstance belonging to the possessive cases of nouns."—*L. Murray's Gram.*, 8vo, p. 53. "*Will*, in the second and third person, only foretels."—*Ib.*, p. 88. "Which seem to form the true distinction between the subjunctive and the indicative moods."—*Ib.*, p. 208. "The very general approbation, which this performance of Walker has received from the public."—*Ib.*, p. 241. "Lest she carry her improvements this way too far."—CAMPBELL: *ib.*, p. 371. "Charles was extravagant, and by this means became poor and despicable."—*Murray's Key*, 8vo, p. 189. "We should entertain no prejudices against simple and rustic persons."—*Ib.*, p. 205. "These are indeed the foundations of all solid merit."—*Blair's Rhet.*, p. 175. "And his embellishment, by means of musical cadence, figures, or other parts of speech."—*Ib.*, p. 175. "If he is at no pains to engage us by the employment of figures, musical arrangement, or any other art of writing."—*Ib.*, p. 181. "The most eminent of the sacred poets are, the Author of the book of Job, David and Isaiah."—*Ib.*, p. 418. "Nothing, in any poet, is more beautifully described than the death of old Priam."—*Ib.*, p. 439. "When two vowels meet together, and are sounded at one breath, they are called *diphthongs*."—*Infant School Gram.*, p. 10. "How many *ss* would goodness then end with? Three."—*Ib.*, p. 33. "*Birds* is a noun, the name of a thing or creature."—*Kirkham's Gram.*, p. 53. "Adam gave names to every living creature."—*Bicknell's Gram.*, Part ii, p. 5. "The steps of a stair ought to be accommodated to the human figure."—*Kames, El. of Crit.*, Vol. ii, p. 337. "Nor ought an emblem more than a simile to be founded on low or familiar objects."—*Ib.*, Vol. ii. p. 357. "Whatever the Latin has not from the Greek, it has from the Goth."—*Tooke's Diversions*, Vol. ii, p. 450. "The mint and secretary of state's offices are neat buildings."—*The Friend*, Vol. iv, p. 266. "The scenes of dead and still life are apt to pall upon us."—*Blair's Rhet.*, p. 407. "And Thomas Aquinas and Duns Scotus, the angelical and the subtle doctors, are the brightest stars in the scholastic constellation."—*Literary Hist.*, p. 244. "The English language has three methods of distinguishing the sex."—*Murray's Gram.*, p. 38; *Ingersoll's*, 27; *Alger's*, 16; *Bacon's*, 13; *Fisk's*, 58; *Greenleaf's*, 21. "The English language has three methods of distinguishing sex."—*Smith's New Gram.*, p. 44. "In English there are the three following methods of distinguishing sex."—*Jaudon's Gram.*, p. 26. "There are three ways of distinguishing the sex."—*Lennie's Gram.*, p. 10; *Picket's*, 26; *Bullions's*, 10. "There are three ways of distinguishing sex."—*Merchant's School Gram.*, p. 26. "Gender is distinguished in three ways."—*Maunder's Gram.*, p. 2. "Neither discourse in general, nor poetry in particular, can be called altogether imitative arts."—*Blair's Rhet.*, p. 51.

"Do we for this the gods and conscience brave,
That one may rule and make the rest a slave?"
—*Rowe's Lucan*, B. ii, l. 96.

LESSON III.—ADJECTIVES.

"There is a deal of more heads, than either heart or horns."—*Barclay's Works*, i, 234.

[FORMULE.—Not proper, because the adjective *more* has not a clear and regular construction, adapted to the author's meaning. But, according to the General Rule of Syntax, "In the formation of sentences, the consistency and adaptation of all the words should be carefully observed; and a regular, clear, and correspondent construction should be preserved throughout." The sentence may be corrected thus: "There is a deal *more* of heads, than *of* either heart or horns."]

"For, of all villains, I think he has the wrong name."—*Bunyan's P. P.*, p. 86. "Of all the men that I met in my pilgrimage, he, I think bears the wrong name."—*Ib.*, p. 84. "I am surprized to see so much of the distribution, and technical terms of the Latin grammar, retained in the grammar of our tongue."—*Priestley's Gram., Pref.*, p. vi. "Nor did the Duke of Burgundy bring him the smallest assistance."—HUME: *Priestley's Gram.*, p. 178. "Else he will find it difficult to make one obstinate believe him."—

Brightland's Gram., p. 243. "Are there any adjectives which form the degrees of comparison peculiar to themselves?"—*Infant School Gram.*, p. 46. "Yet the verbs are all of the indicative mood."—*Lowth's Gram.*, p. 33. "The word *candidate* is in the absolute case."—*L. Murray's Gram.*, 8vo, p. 155. "An Iambus has the first syllable unaccented, and the latter accented."—*Russell's Gram.*, p. 108; *Smith's New Gram.*, 188. "A Dactyl has the first syllable accented, and the two latter unaccented."—*L. Murray*, p. 253; *Bullions's E. Gram.*, 170; *Smith's*, 188; *Kirkham's*, 219; *Guy's*, 120; *Blair's*, 118; *Merchant's*, 167; *Russell's*, 109. "It is proper to begin with a capital the first word of every book, chapter, letter, note, or any other piece of writing."—*L. Murray*, p. 284; *R. C. Smith's New Gram.*, 192; *Ingersoll's*, 295; *Comly's*, 166; *Merchant's*, 14; *Greenleaf's*, 42; *D. C. Allen's*, 85; *Fisk's*, 159; *Bullions's*, 158; *Kirkham's*, 219; *Hiley's*, 119; *Weld's Abridged*, 16; *Bullions's Analyt. and Pract.*, 16; *Fowler's E. Gr.*, 674. "Five and seven make twelve, and one makes thirteen."—*Murray's Key*, 8vo, p. 227. "I wish to cultivate a farther acquaintance with you."—*Ib.*, p. 272. "Let us consider the proper means to effect our purpose."—*Ib.*, p. 276. "Yet they are of such a similar nature, as readily to mix and blend."—*Blair's Rhet.*, p. 48. "The Latin is formed on the same model, but more imperfect."—*Ib.*, p. 83. "I know very well how much pains have been taken."—*Sir W. Temple.* "The management of the breath requires a good deal of care."—*Blair's Rhet.*, p. 331. "Because the mind, during such a momentary stupefaction, is in a good measure, if not totally, insensible."—*Kames, El. of Crit.*, Vol. i, p. 222. "Motives alone of reason and interest are not sufficient."—*Ib.*, Vol. i, p. 232. "To render the composition distinct in its parts, and striking on the whole,"—*Ib.*, Vol. ii, p. 333. "*A* and *an* are named indefinite because they denote some one thing of a kind."—*Maunder's Gram.*, p. 1. "*The* is named definite, because it points out some particular thing."—*Ibid.* "So much depends upon the proper construction of sentences, that, in every sort of composition, we cannot be too strict in our attention to it."—*Blair's Rhet.*,

p. 103. "All sort of declamation and public speaking, was carried on by them."—*Ib.*, p. 123. "The first has on many occasions, a sublimity to which the latter never attains."—*Ib.*, p. 440. "When the words *therefore, consequently, accordingly*, and the like are used in connexion with other conjunctions, they are adverbs."—*Kirkham's Gram.*, p. 88. "Rude nations make little or no allusions to the productions of the arts."—*Jamieson's Rhet.*, p. 10. "While two of her maids knelt on either side of her."—*Mirror*, xi, 307. "The third personal pronouns differ from each other in meaning and use, as follows."—*Bullions, Lat. Gram.*, p. 65. "It was happy for the state, that Fabius continued in the command with Minucius: the former's phlegm was a check upon the latter's vivacity."—*L. Murray's Gram.*, 8vo, p. 57. "If it should be objected that the words must and ought, in the preceding sentences, are all in the present tense."—*Ib.*, p. 108. "But it will be well if you turn to them, every now and then."—*Buckets Classical Gram.*, p. 6. "That every part should have a dependence on, and mutually contribute to support each other."—*Rollin's Hist.*, ii, 115. "The phrase, '*Good, my Lord*,' is not common, and low."—*Priestley's Gram.*, p. 110.

"That brother should not war with brother,
And worry and devour each other."—*Cowper*.

LESSON IV.—PRONOUNS.

"If I can contribute to your and my country's glory."—*Goldsmith*.

[FORMULE.—Not proper, because the pronoun *your* has not a clear and regular construction, adapted to the author's meaning. But, according to the General Rule of Syntax, "In the formation of sentences, the consistency and adaptation of all the words should be carefully observed; and a regular, clear, and correspondent construction should be preserved throughout." The sentence, having a doubtful or double meaning, may be corrected in two ways, thus: "If I can contribute to our country's glory;"—or, "If I can contribute to your *glory* and *that of my country*."]

"As likewise of the several subjects, which have in effect each their verb."—*Lowth's Gram.*, p. 120. "He is likewise required to make examples himself."—*J. Flint's Gram.*, p. 3. "If the emphasis be placed wrong, we shall pervert and confound the meaning wholly."—*Murray's Gram.*, 8vo, p. 242. "If the emphasis be placed wrong, we pervert and confound the meaning wholly."—*Blair's Rhet.*, p. 330. "It was this that characterized the great men of antiquity; it is this, which must distinguish moderns who would tread in their steps."—*Ib.*, p. 341. "I am a great enemy to implicit faith, as well the Popish as Presbyterian, who in that are much what alike."—*Barclay's Works*, iii, 280. "Will he thence dare to say the apostle held another Christ than he that died?"—*Ib.*, iii, 414. "What need you be anxious about this event?"—*Collier's Antoninus*, p. 188. "If a substantive can be placed after the verb, it is active."—*Alex. Murray's Gram.*, p. 31 "When we see bad men honoured and prosperous in the world, it is some discouragement to virtue."—*L. Murray's Key*, 8vo, p. 224. "It is a happiness to young persons, when they are preserved from the snares of the world, as in a garden enclosed."—*Ib.*, p. 171. "The court of Queen Elizabeth, which was but another name for prudence and economy."— *Bullions, E. Gram.*, p. 24. "It is no wonder if such a man did not shine at the court of Queen Elizabeth, who was but another name for prudence and economy. Here which ought to be used, and not who."—*Priestley's Gram.*, p. 99; *Fowler's*, §488. "Better thus; Whose name was but another word for prudence, &c."—*Murray's Gram.*, p. 157; *Fish's*, 115; Ingersoll's, 221; Smith's, 133; and others. "A Defective verb is one that wants some of its parts. They are chiefly the Auxiliary and Impersonal verbs."—*Bullions, E. Gram.*, p. 31; *Old Editions*, 32. "Some writers have given our moods a much greater extent than we have assigned to them."—*Murray's Gram.*, 8vo, p. 67. "The Personal Pronouns give information which no other words are capable of conveying."—*M'Culloch's Gram.*, p. 37, "When the article *a, an,* or *the* precedes the participle, it also becomes a noun."— *Merchant's School Gram.*, p. 93. "There is a preference to be given to some of these, which custom and judgment must determine."—*Murray's Gram.*, 8vo, p. 107. "Many writers affect to subjoin to any word the preposition with which it is compounded, or the idea of which it implies."—*Ib.*, p. 200; *Priestley's Gram.*, 157.

"Say, dost thou know Tectidius?—Who, the wretch
Whose lands beyond the Sabines largely stretch?"
—*Dryden's IV Sat. of Pers.*

LESSON V.—VERBS.

"We would naturally expect, that the word *depend*, would require *from* after it."—*Murray's Gram.*, 8vo, p. 201. "A dish which they pretend to be made of emerald."—*Murray's Key*, 8vo, p. 198. "For the very nature of a sentence implies one proposition to be expressed."—*Blair's Rhet.*, p. 106. "Without a careful attention to the sense, we would be naturally led, by the rules of syntax, to refer it to the rising and setting of the sun."—*Ib.*, p. 105. "For any rules that can be given, on this subject, are very general."—*Ib.*, p. 125. "He is in the right, if eloquence were what he conceives it to be."—*Ib.*, p. 234. "There I would prefer a more free and diffuse manner."—*Ib.*, p. 178. "Yet that they also agreed and resembled one another, in certain qualities."—*Ib.*, p. 73. "But since he must restore her, he insists to have another in her place."—*Ib.*, p. 431. "But these are far from being so frequent or so common as has been supposed."—*Ib.*, p. 445. "We are not misled to assign a wrong place to the pleasant or painful feelings." *Kames, El. of Crit.*, Introd., p. xviii. "Which are of greater importance than is commonly thought."—Vol. ii, p. 92. "Since these qualities are both coarse and common, lets find out the mark of a man of probity."—*Collier's Antoninus*, p. 40. "Cicero did what no man had ever done before him, draw up a treatise of consolation for himself."—*Life of Cicero.* "Then there can be no other Doubt remain of the Truth."—*Brightland's Gram.*, p. 245. "I have observed some satirists use the term."—*Bullions's Prin. of E. Gram.*, p. 79. "Such men are ready to despond, or commence enemies."—*Webster's Essays*, p. 83. "Common nouns express names common to many things."—*Infant School Gram.*, p. 18. "To make ourselves be heard by one to whom we address ourselves."—*Blair's Rhet.*, p. 328. "That, in reading poetry, he may be the better able to judge of its correctness, and relish its beauties."—*Murray's Gram.*, p. 252. "On the stretch to comprehend, and keep pace with the author."— *Blair's Rhet.*, p. 150. "For it might have been sold for more than three hundred pence, and have been given to the poor."—*Mark*, xiv, 5. "He is a beam that is departed, and left no streak of light behind."—OSSIAN: *Kames, El. of Crit.*, ii, 262. "No part of this incident ought to have been represented, but reserved for a narrative."—*Kames, El. of Crit.*, ii, 294. "The rulers and people debauching themselves, brings ruin on a country."—*Ware's Gram.*, p. 9. "When *Doctor, Miss, Master, &c.*, is prefixed to a name, the last of the two words is commonly made plural; as, the *Doctor Nettletons*—the two *Miss Hudsons*."—*Alex. Murray's Gram.*, p. 106. "Wherefore that field was called, The field of blood, unto this day."—*Matt.*, xxvii, 8. "To comprehend the situations of other countries, which perhaps may be necessary for him to explore."—*Brown's Estimate*, ii, 111. "We content ourselves, now, with fewer conjunctive particles than our ancestors did."—*Priestley's Gram.*, p. 139. "And who will be chiefly liable to make mistakes where others have been mistaken before them."—*Ib.*, p. 156. "The voice of nature and revelation unites."—*Wayland's Moral Science*, 3d Ed., p. 307.

"This adjective you see we can't admit,
But changed to *worse,* will make it just and fit."

—*Tobitt's Gram.*, p. 63.

LESSON VI.—PARTICIPLES.

"Its application is not arbitrary, depending on the caprice of readers."—*Murray's Gram.*, 8vo, Vol. i, p. 246. "This is the more expedient, from the work's being designed for the benefit of private learners."—*Ib.*, Vol. ii, p. 161. "A man, he tells us, ordered by his will, to have erected for him a statue."—*Blair's Rhet.*, p. 106. "From some likeness too remote, and laying too far out of the road of ordinary thought."—*Ib.*, p. 146. "Money is a fluid in the commercial world, rolling from hand to hand."—*Webster's Essays*, p. 123. "He pays much attention to learning and singing songs."—*Ib.* p. 246. "I would not be understood to consider singing songs as criminal."—"It is a decided case by the Great Master of writing."—*Preface to Waller*, p. 5. "Did they ever bear a testimony against writing books?"—*Bates's Misc. Repository*. "Exclamations are sometimes mistaking for interrogations."—*Hist. of Printing*, 1770. "Which cannot fail proving of service."—*Smith's Printer's Gram.* "Hewn into such figures as would make them easily and firmly incorporated."—BEATTIE: *Murray's Gram.*, i, 126. "Following the rule and example are practical inductive questions."—*J. Flint's Gram.*, p. 3. "I think there will be an advantage in my having collected examples from modern writings."—*Priestley's Gram.*, Pref., p. xi. "He was eager of recommending it to his fellow-citizens."—HUME: p. 160. "The good lady was careful of serving me of every thing."—"No revelation would have been given, had the light of nature been sufficient in such a sense, as to render one not wanting and useless."—*Butler's Analogy*, p. 155. "Description, again is the raising in the mind the conception of an object by means of some arbitrary or instituted symbols."—*Blair's Rhet.*, p. 52. "Disappointing the expectation of the hearers, when they look for our being done."—*Ib.* p. 326. "There is a distinction which, in the use of them, is deserving of attention."—*Maunder's Gram.*, p. 15. "A model has been contrived, which is not very expensive, and easily managed."—*Education Reporter*. "The conspiracy was the more easily discovered, from its being known to many."—*Murray's Key*, ii, 191. "That celebrated work had been nearly ten years published, before its importance was at all understood."—*Ib.* p. 220. "The sceptre's being ostensibly grasped by a female hand, does not reverse the general order of Government."—*West's Letters to a Lady*, p. 43. "I have hesitated signing the Declaration of Sentiments."—*Liberator*, x, 16. "The prolonging of men's lives when the world needed to be peopled, and now shortening them when that necessity hath ceased to exist."—*Brown's Divinity*, p. 7. "Before the performance commences, we have displayed the insipid formalities of the prelusive scene."—*Kirkham's Elocution*, p. 23. "It forbade the lending of money, or sending goods, or in any way embarking capital in transactions connected with that foreign traffic."—LORD BROUGHAM: *B. and F. Anti-Slavery Reporter*, Vol. ii, p. 218. "Even abstract ideas have sometimes conferred upon them the same important prerogative."—*Jamieson's Rhet.*, p. 171. "Like other terminations, *ment* changes *y* into *i*, when preceded by a consonant."—*Walker's Rhyming Dict.*, p. xiii; *Murray's Gram.*, p. 24: *Ingersoll's*, 11. "The term *proper* is from being *proper*, that is, *peculiar* to the individual bearing the name. The term *common* is from being *common* to every individual comprised in the class."—*Fowler's E. Gram.*, 8vo, 1850, §139.

"Thus oft by mariners are shown (Unless the men of Kent are liars)
Earl Godwin's castles overflown, And palace-roofs, and steeple-spires."
—*Swift*, p. 313.

LESSON VII.—ADVERBS.

"He spoke to every man and woman there."—*Murray's Gram.*, p. 220; *Fisk's*, 147. "Thought and language act and react upon each other mutually."—*Blair's Rhet.*, p. 120; *Murray's Exercises*, 133. "Thought and expression act upon each other mutually."—See *Murray's Key*, p. 264. "They have neither the leisure nor the means of attaining scarcely any knowledge, except what lies within the contracted circle of their several professions."—*Murray's Gram.*, 8vo, p. 359. "Before they are capable of understanding but little, or indeed any thing of many other branches of education."—*Olney's Introd. to Geog.*, p. 5. "There is not more beauty in one of them than in another."—*Murray's Key*, ii, 275. "Which appear not constructed according to any certain rule."—*Blair's Rhet.*, p. 47. "The vehement manner of speaking became not so universal."—*Ib.*, p. 61. "All languages, however, do not agree in this mode of expression."—*Ib.*, p. 77. "The great occasion of setting aside this particular day."—ATTERBURY: p. 294. "He is much more promising now than formerly."—*Murray's Gram.*, Vol. ii, p. 4. "They are placed before a participle, independently on the rest of the sentence."—*Ib.*, Vol. ii, p. 21. "This opinion appears to be not well considered."—*Ib.*, Vol. i, p. 153; *Ingersoll's*, 249. "Precision in language merits a full explication; and the more, because distinct ideas are, perhaps, not commonly formed about it."—*Blair's Rhet.*, p. 94. "In the more sublime parts of poetry, he [Pope] is not so distinguished."—*Ib.*, p. 403. "How far the author was altogether happy in the choice of his subject, may be questioned."—*Ib.*, p. 450. "But here also there is a great error in the common practice."—*Webster's Essays*, p. 7. "This order is the very order of the human mind, which makes things we are sensible of, a means to come at those that are not so."—*Formey's Belles-Lettres, Foreman's Version*, p. 113. "Now, Who is not Discouraged, and Fears Want, when he has no money?"—*Divine Right of Tythes*, p. 23. "Which the Authors of this work, consider of but little or no use."—*Wilbur and Livingston's Gram.*, p. 6. "And here indeed the distinction between these two classes begins not to be clear."—*Blair's Rhet.*, p. 152. "But this is a manner which deserves not to be imitated."—*Ib.*, p. 180. "And in this department a person never effects so little, as when he attempts too much."—*Campbell's Rhet.*, p. 173; *Murray's Gram.*, 8vo, p. 367. "The verb that signifies merely being, is neuter."—*Dr. Ash's Gram.*, p. 27. "I hope not much to tire those whom I shall not happen to please."—*Rambler*, No. 1. "Who were utterly unable to pronounce some letters, and others very indistinctly."—*Sheridan's Elocution*, p. 32. "The learner may point out the active, passive, and neuter verbs in the following examples, and state the reasons why."—*C. Adams's Gram.*, p. 27. "These words are most always conjunctions."—*S. Barrett's Revised Gram.*, p. 73.

"How fluent nonsense trickles from his tongue!
How sweet the periods, neither said, nor sung!"—*Dunciad.*

LESSON VIII.—CONJUNCTIONS.

"Who at least either knew not, nor loved to make, a distinction."—*Dr. Murray's Hist. of Europ. Lang.*, i, 322. "It is childish in the last degree, if this become the ground of estranged affection."—*L. Murray's Key*, ii, 228. "When the regular or the irregular verb is to be preferred, p. 107."—*Murray's Index, Gram.*, ii, 296. "The books were to have been sold, as this day."—*Priestley's E. Gram.*, p. 138. "Do, an if you will."—*Beauties of Shak.*, p. 195. "If a man had a positive idea of infinite, either duration or space, he could add two infinites together."—*Murray's Gram.*, 8vo, p. 174. "None shall more willingly agree and advance the same nor I."—EARL OF MORTON: *Robertson's Scotland*, ii, 428. "That it cannot be but hurtful to continue it."—*Barclay's Works*, i, 192. "A conjunction joins words and sentences."—*Beck's Gram.*, pp. 4 and 25. "The copulative conjunction connects words and sentences together and continues the sense."—*Frost's El. of Gram.*, p. 42. "The Conjunction Copulative serves to connect or continue a sentence, by expressing an addition, a supposition, a cause, &c."—*Murray's Gram.*, 8vo, i, 123. "All Construction is either true or apparent; or in other Words just and figurative."—*Buchanan's Syntax*, p. 130; *British Gram.*, 234. "But the divine character is such that none but a divine hand could draw."—*The Friend*, Vol. v, p. 72. "Who is so mad, that, on inspecting the heavens, is insensible of a God?"—CICERO:—*Dr. Gibbons.* "It is now submitted to an enlightened public, with little desire on the part of the Author, than its general utility."—*Town's Analysis*, 9th Ed., p. 5. "This will sufficiently explain the reason, that so many provincials have grown old in the capital without making any change in their original dialect."—*Sheridan's Elocution*, p. 51. "Of these they had chiefly three in general use, which were denominated accents, and the term used in the plural number."—*Ib.*, p. 56. "And this is one of the chief reasons, that dramatic representations have ever held the first rank amongst the diversions of mankind."—*Ib.*, p. 95. "Which is the chief reason that public reading is in general so disgusting."—*Ib.*, p. 96. "At the same time that they learn to read."—*Ib.*, p. 96. "He is always to pronounce his words exactly with the same accent that he speaks them."—*Ib.*, p. 98. "In order to know what another knows, and in the same manner that he knows it."—*Ib.*, p. 136. "For the same reason that it is in a more limited state assigned to the several tribes of animals."—*Ib.*, p. 145. "Were there masters to teach this, in the same manner as other arts are taught."—*Ib.*, p. 169.

"Whose own example strengthens all his laws;
And is himself that great Sublime he draws."—*Pope, on Crit.*, l. 680.

LESSON IX.—PREPOSITIONS.

"The word *so* has, sometimes, the same meaning with *also, likewise, the same.*"—*Priestley's Gram.*, p. 137. "The verb *use* relates not to pleasures of the imagination, but to the terms of fancy and imagination, which he was to employ as synonymous."—*Blair's Rhet.*, p. 197. "It never can view, clearly and distinctly, above one object at a time."—*Ib.*, p. 94. "This figure [Euphemism] is often the same with the Periphrasis."—*Adam's Gram.*, p. 247; *Gould's*, 238. "All the between time of youth and old age."—*Walker's Particles*, p. 83. "When one thing is said to act upon, or do something to another."—*Lowth's Gram.*, p. 70. "Such a composition has as much of meaning in it, as a mummy has life."—*Journal of Lit. Convention*, p. 81. "That young men of from fourteen to eighteen were not the best judges."—*Ib.*, p. 130. "This day is a day of trouble, and of rebuke, and blasphemy."—*2 Kings*, xix, 3. "Blank verse has the same pauses and accents with rhyme."—*Kames, El. of Crit.*, ii, 119. "In prosody, long syllables are distinguished by ([=]), and short ones by what is called *breve* ([~])."—*Bucke's Gram.*, p. 22. "Sometimes both articles are left out, especially in poetry."—*Ib.*, p. 26. "In the following example, the pronoun and participle are omitted: [*He being*] 'Conscious of his own weight and importance, the aid of others was not solicited.'"—*Murray's Gram.*, 8vo, p. 221. "He was an excellent person; a mirror of ancient faith in early youth."—*Murray's Key*, 8vo, p. 172. "The carrying on its several parts into execution."—*Butler's Analogy*, p. 192. "Concord, is the agreement which one word has over another, in gender, number, case, and person."—*Folker's Gram.*, p. 3. "It might perhaps have given me a greater taste of its antiquities."— ADDISON: *Priestley's Gram.*, p. 160. "To call of a person, and to wait of him."—*Priestley, ib.*, p. 161. "The great difficulty they found of fixing just sentiments."—HUME: *ib.*, p. 161. "Developing the difference between the three."—*James Brown's first American Gram.*, p. 12. "When the substantive singular ends in *x*, *ch* soft, *sh*, *ss*, or *s*, we add *es* in the plural."—*Murray's Gram.*, p. 40. "We shall present him with a list or specimen of them."—*Ib.*, p. 132. "It is very common to hear of the evils of pernicious reading, of how it enervates the mind, or how it depraves the principles."—*Dymond's*

Essays, p. 168. "In this example, the verb 'arises' is understood before 'curiosity' and 'knowledge.'"—*Murray's Gram.*, 8vo, p. 274; *Ingersoll's*, 286; *Comly's*, 155; and others. "The connective is frequently omitted between several words."—*Wilcox's Gram.*, p. 81. "He shall expel them from before you, and drive them from out of your sight."—*Joshua*, xxiii, 5. "Who makes his sun shine and his rain to descend upon the just and the unjust."—*M'Ilvaine's Lectures*, p. 411.

LESSON X.—MIXED EXAMPLES.

"This sentence violates the rules of grammar."—*Murray's Gram.*, 8vo, Vol. ii, pp. 19 and 21. "The words *thou* and *shalt* are again reduced to short quantities."—*Ib.*, Vol. i, p. 246. "Have the greater men always been the most popular? By no means."—DR. LIEBER: *Lit. Conv.*, p. 64. "St. Paul positively stated that, 'he who loves one another has fulfilled the law.'"—*Spurzheim, on Education*, p. 248. "More than one organ is concerned in the utterance of almost every consonant."—*M'Culloch's Gram.*, p. 18. "If the reader will pardon my descending so low."—*Campbell's Rhet.*, p. 20. "To adjust them so, as shall consist equally with the perspicuity and the grace of the period."—*Blair's Rhet.*, p. 118: *Murray's Gram.*, 8vo, p. 324. "This class exhibits a lamentable want of simplicity and inefficiency."—*Gardiner's Music of Nature*, p. 481. "Whose style flows always like a limpid stream, where we see to the very bottom."—*Blair's Rhet.*, p. 93. "Whose style flows always like a limpid stream, through which we see to the very bottom."—*Murray's Gram.*, 8vo, p. 293. "We make use of the ellipsis." [447]—*Ib.*, p. 217. "The ellipsis of the article is thus used."—*Ib.*, p. 217. "Sometimes the ellipsis is improperly applied to nouns of different numbers: as, 'A magnificent house and gardens.'"—*Ib.*, p. 218. "In some very emphatic expressions, the ellipsis should not be used."—*Ib.*, 218. "The ellipsis of the adjective is used in the following manner."—*Ib.*, 218. "The following is the ellipsis of the pronoun."—*Ib.*, 218. "The ellipsis of the verb is used in the following instances."—*Ib.*, p. 219. "The ellipsis of the adverb is used in the following manner."—*Ib.*, 219. "The following instances, though short, contain much of the ellipsis."—*Ib.*, 220. "If no emphasis be placed on any words, not only will discourse be rendered heavy and lifeless, but the meaning often ambiguous."—*Ib.*, 242. See *Hart's Gram.*, p. 172. "If no emphasis be placed on any words, not only is discourse, rendered heavy and lifeless, but the meaning left often ambiguous."—*Blair's Rhet.*, p. 330; *Murray's Eng. Reader*, p. xi. "He regards his word, but thou dost not regard it."—*Bullions's E. Gram.*, p. 129; *his Analytical and Practical Gram.*, p. 196. "He regards his word, but thou dost not: i.e. dost not regard it."—*Murray's Gram.*, 8vo, p. 219; *Parker and Fox's*, p. 96; *Weld's*, 192. "I have learned my task, but you have not; i.e. have not learned."—*Ib.*, *Mur.*, 219; &c. "When the omission of words would obscure the sentence, weaken its force, or be attended with an impropriety, they must be expressed."—*Ib.*, p. 217; *Weld's Gram.* 190. "And therefore the verb is correctly put in the singular number, and refers to the whole separately and individually considered."—*Murray's Gram.* 8vo, ii, 24 and 190. "I understood him the best of all who spoke on the subject."—*Murray's Key*, 8vo, p. 192. "I understood him better than any other who spoke on the subject."—*Ibid.*, "The roughness found on our entrance into the paths of virtue and learning, grow smoother as we advance."—*Ib.*, p. 171. "The roughnesses," &c.—*Murray's Key*, 12mo, p 8. "Nothing promotes knowledge more than steady application, and a habit of observation."—*Murray's Key*, 8vo, p. 265. "Virtue confers supreme dignity on man: and should be his chief desire."—*Ib.*, p. 192; *and Merchant's*, 192. "The Supreme author of our being has so formed the soul of man, that nothing but himself can be its last, adequate, and proper happiness."—*Addison, Spect.*, No. 413; *Blair's Rhet.*, p. 213. "The inhabitants of China laugh at the plantations of our Europeans; because, they say, any one may place trees in equal rows and uniform figures."—*Ad., Spect.*, No. 414; *Blair's Rhet.*, p. 222. "The divine laws are not reversible by those of men."—*Murray's Key*, ii, 167. "In both of these examples, the relative and the verb *which was*, are understood."—*Murray's Gram.*, p. 273; *Comly's*, 152; *Ingersoll's*, 285. "The Greek and Latin languages, though, for many reasons, they cannot be called dialects of one another, are nevertheless closely connected."—*Dr. Murray's Hist. of European Lang.*, Vol. ii, p. 51. "To ascertain and settle which, of a white rose or a red rose, breathes the sweetest fragrance."—*J. Q. Adams, Orat.*, 1831. "To which he can afford to devote much less of his time and labour."—*Blair's Rhet.*, p. 254.

"Avoid extremes; and shun the fault of such,
  Who still are pleas'd too little or too much."
      —*Pope, on Crit.*, 1, 384.

LESSON XI.—BAD PHRASES.

"He had as good leave his vessel to the direction of the winds."—SOUTH: *in Joh. Dict.* "Without good nature and gratitude, men had as good live in a wilderness as in society."—L'ESTRANGE: *ib.* "And for this reason such lines almost never occur together."—*Blair's Rhet.*, p. 385. "His being a great man did not make him a happy man."—*Crombie's Treatise*, p. 288. "Let that which tends to the making cold your love be judged in all."—*S. Crisp.* "It is worthy the observing, that there is no passion in the mind of man so weak but it mates and masters the fear of death."—*Bacon's Essays*, p. 4. "Accent dignifies the syllable on which it is laid, and makes it more distinguished by the ear than the rest."—*Sheridan's Lect.*, p. 80; *Murray's Gram.*, 8vo, p. 244. "Before he proceeds to argue either on one side or other."—*Blair's Rhet.*, p. 313. "The change in general of manners throughout all Europe."—*Ib.*, p. 375. "The sweetness and beauty of Virgil's numbers, throughout his whole works."—*Ib.*, p. 440. "The French writers of sermons study neatness and elegance in laying down their heads."—*Ib.*, p. 13. "This almost never fails to prove a refrigerant to passion."—*Ib.*, p. 321. "At least their fathers, brothers, and uncles, cannot, as good relations and good citizens, dispense with their not standing forth to demand vengeance."—*Goldsmith's Greece*, Vol. i, p. 191. "Alleging, that their crying down the church of Rome, was a joining hand with the Turks."—*Barclay's Works*, i, 239. "To which is added the Assembly of Divines Catechism."—*New-England Primer*, p. 1. "This treachery was always present in both their thoughts."—*Dr. Robertson.* "Thus far both their words agree." ("*Convenient adhuo utriusqus verba.* Plaut.")—*Walker's Particles*, p. 125. "Aparithmesis, or Enumeration, is the branching out into several parts of what might be expressed in fewer words."—*Gould's Gram*, p. 241. "Aparithmesis, or Enumeration, is when what might be expressed in a few words, is branched out into several parts."—*Adam's Gram.*, p. 251. "Which may sit from time to time where you dwell or in the neighbouring vicinity."—*Taylor's District School*, 1st Ed., p. 281. "Place together a large and a small sized animal of the same species."—*Kames, El. of Crit.*, i, 235. "The weight of the swimming body is equal to that of the weight, of the quantity of fluid displaced by it."—*Percival's Tales*, ii, 213. "The Subjunctive mood, in all its tenses, is similar to that of the Optative."—*Gwilt's Saxon Gram.*, p. 27. "No other feeling of obligation remains, except that of fidelity."—*Wayland's Moral Science*, 1st Ed., p. 82. "Who asked him, 'What could be the reason, that whole audiences should be moved to tears, at the representation of some story on the stage.'"—*Sheridan's Elocution*, p. 175. "Art not thou and you ashamed to affirm, that the best works of the Spirit of Christ in his saints are as filthy rags?"—*Barclay's Works*, i, 174. "A neuter verb becomes active, when followed by a noun of the same signification with its own."—*Sanborn's Gram.*, p. 127. "But he has judged better, in omitting to repeat the article *the*."—*Blair's Rhet.*, p.

194. "Many objects please us as highly beautiful, which have almost no variety at all."—*Ib.*, p. 46. "Yet notwithstanding, they sometimes follow them."—*Emmons's Gram.*, p. 21. "For I know of nothing more material in all the whole Subject, than this doctrine of Mood and Tense."—*Johnson's Gram. Com.*, p. 292. "It is by no means impossible for an errour to be got rid of or supprest."— *Philological Museum*, Vol. i, p. 642. "These are things of the highest importance to the growing age."—*Murray's Key*, 8vo, p. 250. "He had better have omitted the word *many*."—*Blair's Rhet.* p. 205. "Which had better have been separated."—*Ib.*, p. 225. "Figures and metaphors, therefore, should, on no occasion be stuck on too profusely."—*Ib.*, p. 144; *Jamieson's Rhet.*, 150. "Metaphors, as well as other figures, should on no occasion, be stuck on too profusely."—*Murray's Gram.*, p. 338; *Russell's*, 136. "Something like this has been reproached to Tacitus."—BOLINGBROKE: *Priestley's Gram.*, p. 164.

"O thou, whom all mankind in vain withstand,
Each of whose blood must one day stain thy hand!"
   —*Sheffield's Temple of Death.*

LESSON XII.—TWO ERRORS.[448]

"Pronouns are sometimes made to precede the things which they represent."—*Murray's Gram.*, p. 160. "Most prepositions originally denote the relation of place."—*Lowth's Gram.*, p. 65. "*Which* is applied to inferior animals and things without life."—*Bullions, E. Gram.*, p. 24; *Pract. Lessons*, 30. "What noun do they describe or tell the kind?"—*Infant School Gram.*, p. 41. "Iron cannon, as well as brass, is now universally cast solid."—*Jamieson's Dict.* "We have philosophers, eminent and conspicuous, perhaps, beyond any nation."—*Blair's Rhet.*, p. 251. "This is a question about words alone, and which common sense easily determines."—*Ib.*, p.

320. "The low [pitch of the voice] is, when he approaches to a whisper."—*Ib.*, p. 328. "Which, as to the effect, is just the same with using no such distinctions at all."—*Ib.*, p. 33. "These two systems, therefore, differ in reality very little from one another."—*Ib.*, p. 23. "It were needless to give many instances, as they occur so often."—*Ib.*, p. 109. "There are many occasions when this is neither requisite nor would be proper."—*Ib.*, p. 311. "Dramatic poetry divides itself into the two forms, of comedy or tragedy."—*Ib.*, p. 452. "No man ever rhymed truer and evener than he."—*Pref. to Waller*, p. 5. "The Doctor did not reap a profit from his poetical labours equal to those of his prose."—*Johnson's Life of Goldsmith*. "We will follow that which we found our fathers practice."—*Sale's Koran*, i, 28. "And I would deeply regret having published them."—*Infant School Gram.*, p. vii. "Figures exhibit ideas in a manner more vivid and impressive, than could be done by plain language."—*Kirkham's Gram.*, p. 222. "The allegory is finely drawn, only the heads various."—*Spect.*, No. 540. "I should not have thought it worthy a place here."—*Crombie's Treatise*, p. 219. "In this style, Tacitus excels all writers, ancient and modern."—*Kames, El. of Crit.*, ii, 261. "No author, ancient or modern, possesses the art of dialogue equal to Shakspeare."—*Ib.*, ii, 294. "The names of every thing we hear, see, smell, taste, and feel, are nouns."—*Infant School Gram.*, p. 16. "What number are these boys? these pictures? &c."—*Ib.*, p. 23. "This sentence is faulty, somewhat in the same manner with the last."—*Blair's Rhet.*, p. 230. "Besides perspicuity, he pursues propriety, purity, and precision, in his language; which forms one degree, and no inconsiderable one, of beauty."—*Ib.*, p. 181. "Many critical terms have unfortunately been employed in a sense too loose and vague; none more so, than that of the sublime."—*Ib.*, p. 35. "Hence, no word in the language is used in a more vague signification than beauty."—*Ib.*, p. 45. "But, still, he made use only of general terms in speech."—*Ib.*, p. 73. "These give life, body, and colouring to the recital of facts, and enable us to behold them as present,

and passing before our eyes."—*Ib.*, p. 360. "Which carried an ideal chivalry to a still more extravagant height than it had risen in fact."—*Ib.*, p. 374. "We write much more supinely, and at our ease, than the ancients."—*Ib.*, p. 351. "This appears indeed to form the characteristical difference between the ancient poets, orators, and historians, compared with the modern."—*Ib.*, p. 350. "To violate this rule, as is too often done by the English, shews great incorrectness."— *Ib.*, p. 463. "It is impossible, by means of any study to avoid their appearing stiff and forced."—*Ib.*, p. 335. "Besides its giving the speaker the disagreeable appearance of one who endeavours to compel assent."—*Ib.*, p. 328. "And, on occasions where a light or ludicrous anecdote is proper to be recorded, it is generally better to throw it into a note, than to hazard becoming too familiar."—*Ib.*, p. 359. "The great business of this life is to prepare, and qualify us, for the enjoyment of a better."—*Murray's Gram.*, 8vo, p. 373. "In some dictionaries, accordingly, it was omitted; and in others stigmatized as a barbarism."— *Crombie's Treatise*, p. 322. "You cannot see, or think of, a thing, unless it be a noun."—*Mack's Gram.*, p. 65. "The fleet are all arrived and moored in safety."—*Murray's Key*, ii, 185.

LESSON XIII.—TWO ERRORS.

"They have each their distinct and exactly-limited relation to gravity."—*Hasler's Astronomy*, p 219. "But in cases which would give too much of the hissing sound, the omission takes place even in prose."—*Murray's Gram.*, 8vo, p. 175. "After *o* it [the *w*] is sometimes not sounded at all; sometimes like a single *u*."—*Lowth's Gram.*, p. 3. "It is situation chiefly which decides *of* the fortunes and characters of men."—HUME: *Priestley's Gram.*, p. 159. "It is situation chiefly which decides the fortune (or, *concerning* the fortune) and characters of men."—*Murray's Gram.*, 8vo, p. 201. "The vice of covetousness is what enters deeper into the soul than any other."—*Ib.*, p.

167; *Ingersoll's*, 193; *Fisk's*, 103; *Campbell's Rhet.*, 205. "Covetousness, of all vices, enters the deepest into the soul."—*Murray*, 167; *and others.* "Covetousness is what of all vices enters the deepest into the soul."—*Campbell's Rhet.*, p. 205. "The vice of covetousness is what enters deepest into the soul of any other."—*Guardian*, No. 19. "*Would* primarily denotes inclination of will; and *should*, obligation; but they both vary their import, and are often used to express simple event."—*Lowth's Gram.*, p. 43; *Murray's*, 89; *Fisk's*, 78; *Greenleaf's*, 27. "But they both vary their import, and are often used to express simple events."—*Comly's Gram.*, p. 39; *Ingersoll's*, 137. "But they vary their import, and are often used to express simple event."—*Abel Flint's Gram.*, p 42. "A double conjunctive, in two correspondent clauses of a sentence, is sometimes made use of: as, '*Had* he done this, he *had* escaped.'"—*Murray's Gram.*, 8vo, p. 213; *Ingersoll's*, 269. "The pleasures of the understanding are preferable to those of the imagination, or of sense."—*Murray's Key*, 8vo, p. 191. "Claudian, in a fragment upon the wars of the giants, has contrived to render this idea of their throwing the mountains, which is in itself so grand, burlesque, and ridiculous."—*Blair's Rhet.*, p. 42. "To which not only no other writings are to be preferred, but even in divers respects not comparable."— *Barclay's Works*, i, 53. "To distinguish them in the understanding, and treat of their several natures, in the same cool manner as we do with regard to other ideas."—*Sheridan's Elocution*, p. 137. "For it has nothing to do with parsing, or analyzing, language."—*Kirkham's Gram.*, p. 19. Or: "For it has nothing to do with parsing, or analyzing, language."—*Ib.*, *Second Edition*, p. 16. "Neither was that language [the Latin] ever so vulgar in Britain."— SWIFT: see *Blair's Rhet.*, p. 228. "All that I propose is to give some openings into the pleasures of taste."—*Ib.*, p. 28. "But it would have been better omitted in the following sentences."—*Murray's Gram.*, 8vo, p. 210. "But I think it had better be omitted in the following sentence."—*Priestley's Gram.*, p. 162. "They appear, in this case, like excrescences jutting out from the body, which had better have been wanted."—*Blair's Rhet.*, p. 326. "And therefore, the fable of the Harpies, in the third book of the Æneid, and the allegory of Sin and Death, in the second book of Paradise Lost, had been better omitted in these celebrated poems."—*Ib.*, p. 430. "Ellipsis is an elegant Suppression (or the leaving out) of a Word, or Words in a Sentence."—*British Gram.*, p. 234; *Buchanan's*, p. 131. "The article *a* or *an* had better be omitted in this construction."—*Blair's Gram.*, p. 67. "Now suppose the articles had not been left out in these passages."—*Burke's Gram.*, p. 27. "To give separate names to every one of those trees, would have been an endless and impracticable undertaking."—*Blair's Rhet.*, p. 72. "*Ei*, in general, sounds the same as long and slender *a*."—*Murray's Gram.*, p. 12. "When a conjunction is used apparently redundant it is called Polysyndeton."—*Adam's Gram.*, p. 236; *Gould's*, 229. "*Each, every, either, neither*, denote the persons or things which make up a number, as taken separately or distributively."— *M'Culloch's Gram.*, p. 31. "The Principal Sentence must be expressed by verbs in the Indicative, Imperative, or Potential Modes."—*Clark's Pract. Gram.*, p. 133. "Hence he is diffuse, where he ought to have been pressing."—*Blair's Rhet.*, p. 246. "All manner of subjects admit of explaining comparisons."—*Ib.*, p. 164; *Jamieson's Rhet.*, 161. "The present or imperfect participle denotes action or being continued, but not perfected."—*Kirkham's Gram.*, p. 78. "What are verbs? Those words which express what the nouns do"—*Fowle's True Eng. Gram.*, p. 29.

"Of all those arts in which the wise excel,
Nature's chief masterpiece is writing well."
—*J. Sheffield, Duke of Buck.*

"Such was that muse whose rules and practice tell
Nature's chief masterpiece is writing well."
—*Pope, on Criticism.*

LESSON XIV.—THREE ERRORS.

"In some words the metaphorical sense has justled out the original sense altogether, so that in respect of it they are become obsolete."— *Campbell's Rhet.*, p. 323. "Sure never any mortal was so overwhelmed with grief as I am at this present."—*Sheridan's Elocution,* p. 138. "All languages differ from each other in their mode of inflexion."—*Bullions, E. Gram.*, Pref., p. v. "Nouns and verbs are the only indispensable parts of speech—the one to express the subject spoken of, and the other the predicate or what is affirmed of it."—*M'Culloch's Gram.*, p. 36. "The words in italics of the three latter examples, perform the office of substantives."—*L. Murray's Gram.*, 8vo, p. 66. "Such a structure of a sentence is always the mark of careless writing."—*Blair's Rhet.*, p. 231. "Nothing is frequently more hurtful to the grace or vivacity of a period, than superfluous dragging words at the conclusion."—*Ib.*, p. 205. "When its substantive is not joined to it, but referred to, or understood."— *Lowth's Gram.*, p. 24. "Yet they have always some substantive belonging to them, either referred to, or understood."—*Ib.*, 24. "Because they define and limit the extent of the common name, or general term, to which they either refer, or are joined.'"— *Ib.*, 24. "Every new object surprises, terrifies, and makes a strong impression on their mind."—*Blair's Rhet.*, p. 136. "His argument required to have been more fully unfolded, in order to make it be distinctly apprehended, and to give it its due force."—*Ib.*, p. 230. "Participles which are derived from active verbs, will govern the objective case, the same as the verbs from which they are derived"—*Emmons's Gram.*, p. 61. "Where, contrary to the rule, the nominative *I* precedes, and the objective case *whom* follows the verb."—*Murray's Gram.*, 8vo, p. 181. "The same conjunction governing both the indicative and the subjunctive moods, in the same sentence, and in the same circumstances, seems to be a great impropriety."—*Ib.*, p. 207; *Smith's New Gram.*, 173: see *Lowth's Gram.*, p. 105; *Fisk's*, 128; and *Ingersoll's*, 266. "A nice discernment, and accurate attention to the best usage, are necessary to direct us, on these occasions."—*Murray's Gram.*, 8vo, p. 170. "The Greeks and Romans, the former especially, were, in truth, much more musical nations than we; their genius was more turned to delight in the melody of speech."—*Blair's Rhet.*, p. 123. "When the sense admits it, the sooner a circumstance is introduced, the better, that the more important and significant words may possess the last place, quite disencumbered."—*Murray's Gram.*, 8vo, i, p. 309; *Parker and Fox's*, Part III, p. 88. "When the sense admits it, the sooner they are despatched, generally speaking, the better; that the more important and significant words may possess the last place, quite disencumbered."— *Blair's Rhet.*, p. 118. See also *Jamieson's Rhet.*, p. 101. "Thus we find it, both in the Greek and Latin tongues."—*Blair's Rhet.*, p. 74. "A train of sentences, constructed in the same manner, and with the same number of members, should never be allowed to succeed one another."—*Ib.*, p. 102; *Murray's Gram.*, 8vo, Vol. i, p. 306; *Parker and Fox's Gram.*, Part III, p. 86. "I proceed to lay down the rules to be observed in the conduct of metaphors, and which are much the same for tropes of every kind."—*Blair's Rhet.*, p. 143. "By a proper choice of words, we may produce a resemblance of other sounds which we mean to describe."—*Ib.*, p. 129; *Murray's Gram.*, 8vo, Vol. i, p. 331. "The disguise can almost never be so perfect, but it is discovered."—*Blair's Rhet.*, p. 259. "The sense admits of no other pause than after the second syllable 'sit,' which therefore must be the only pause made in the reading."—*Ib.*, p. 333. "Not that I believe North America to be peopled so late as the twelfth century, the period of Madoc's migration."— *Webster's Essays*, p. 212. "Money and commodities will always flow to that country, where they are most wanted and will command the most profit."— *Ib.*, p. 308. "That it contains no visible marks, of articles, which are the most important of all others, to a just delivery."— *Sheridan's Elocution*, p. 13. "And of virtue, from its beauty, we call it a fair and favourite maid."—

Mack's Gram., p. 66. "The definite article may agree with nouns in the singular and plural number."—*Infant School Gram.*, p. 130.

LESSON XV.—MANY ERRORS.

(1.) "A compound word is included under the head of derivative words."—*Murray's Gram.*, 8vo, p. 23. (2.) "An Apostrophe, marked thus ' is used to abbreviate or shorten a word. Its chief use is to show the genitive case of nouns."—*Ib.*, p. 281.[449] (3.) "A Hyphen, marked thus - is employed in connecting compounded words. It is also used when a word is divided."—*Ib.*, p. 282. (4.) "The Acute Accent, marked thus ´: as, '*Fáncy*.' The Grave thus ` as, '*Fàvour*'"—*Ib.*, p. 282. (5.) "The stress is laid on long and short syllables indiscriminately. In order to distinguish the one from the other, some writers of dictionaries have placed the grave on the former, and the acute on the latter."—*Ib.*, 282. (6.) "A Diæresis, thus marked ¨, consists of two points placed over one of the two vowels that would otherwise make a diphthong, and parts them into syllables."—*Ib.*, 282. (7.) "A Section marked thus §, is the division of a discourse, or chapter, into less parts or portions."—*Ib.*, 282. (8.) "A Paragraph ¶ denotes the beginning of a new subject, or a sentence not connected with the foregoing. This character is chiefly used in the Old and in the New Testaments."—*Ib.*, 282. (9.) "A Quotation " ". Two inverted commas are generally placed at the beginning of a phrase or a passage, which is quoted or transcribed from the speaker or author in his own words; and two commas in their direct position, are placed at the conclusion."—*Ib.*, 282. (10.) "A Brace is used in poetry at the end of a triplet or three lines, which have the same rhyme. Braces are also used to connect a number of words with one common term, and are introduced to prevent a repetition in writing or printing."—*Ib.*, p. 283. (11.) "Two or three asterisks generally denote the omission of some letters in a word, or of some bold or indelicate expression, or some defect in the manuscript."—*Ib.*, 283. (12.) "An Ellipsis —— is also used, when some letters in a word, or some words in a verse, are omitted."—*Ib.*, 283. (13.) "An Obelisk, which is marked thus [dagger], and Parallels thus ‖, together with the letters of the Alphabet, and figures, are used as references to the margin, or bottom of the page."—*Ib.*, 283. (14.) "A note of interrogation should not be employed, in cases where it is only said a question has been asked, and where the words are not used as a question. 'The Cyprians asked me why I wept.'"—*Ib.*, p. 279; *Comly*, 163; *Ingersoll*, 291; *Fisk*, 157; *Flint*, 113. (15.) "A point of interrogation is improper after sentences which are not questions, but only expressions of admiration, or of some other emotion."—*Same authors and places*. (16.) "The parenthesis incloses in the body of a sentence a member inserted into it, which is neither necessary to the sense, nor at all affects the construction."—*Lowth's Gram.*, p. 124. (17.) "Simple members connected by relatives, and comparatives, are for the most part distinguished by a comma." [450]—*Ib.*, p. 121. (18.) "Simple members of sentences connected by comparatives, are, for the most part, distinguished by a comma."—*L. Murray's Gram.*, p 272; *Alden's*, 148; *Ingersoll's*, 284. See the same words without the last two commas, in *Comly's Gram.*, p. 149; *Alger's*, 79; *Merchant's Murray*, 143:—and this again, with a *different sense*, made by a comma before "*connected*," in *Smith's New Gram.*, 190; *Abel Flint's*, 103. (19.) "Simple members of sentences connected by comparatives, are for the most part distinguished by the comma."—*Russell's Gram.*, p. 115. (20.) "Simple members of sentences, connected by comparatives, should generally be distinguished by a comma."—*Merchant's School Gram.*, p. 150. (21.) "Simple members of sentences connected by *than* or *so*, or that express contrast or comparison, should, generally, be divided by a comma."—*Jaudon's Gram.*, p. 185. (22.) "Simple members of sentences, connected by comparatives, if they be long, are separated by a comma."—*Cooper's New Gram.*, p. 195. See the same without the first comma, in *Cooper's Murray*, p. 183. (23.) "Simple members of sentences connected by comparatives, and phrases placed in opposition to, or in contrast with, each other, are separated by commas."—*Bullions*, p. 153; *Hiley*, 113. (24.) "On which ever word we lay the emphasis, whether on the first, second, third, or fourth, it strikes out a different sense."—*Murray's Gram.*, 8vo, p. 243. (25.) "To inform those who do not understand sea phrases, that, 'We tacked to the larboard, and stood off to sea,' would be expressing ourselves very obscurely."—*Ib.*, p. 296; *and Hiley's Gram.*, p. 151. (26.) "Of dissyllables, which are at once nouns and verbs, the verb has commonly the accent on the latter, and the noun, on the former syllable."—*Murray*, p. 237. (27.) "And this gives our language a superior advantage to most others, in the poetical and rhetorical style."—*Id. ib.*, p. 38; *Ingersoll*, 27; *Fisk*, 57. (28.) "And this gives the English an advantage above most other languages in the poetical and rhetorical style."—*Lowth's Gram*, p. 19. (29.) "The second and third scholar may read the same sentence; and as many, as it is necessary to learn it perfectly to the whole."—*Osborn's Key*, p. 4.

(30.) "Bliss is the name in subject as a king,
　　In who obtain defence, or who defend."
　　　—*Bullions, E. Gram.*, p. 178.

LESSON XVI.—MANY ERRORS.

"The Japanese, the Tonquinese, and the Corceans, speak different languages from one another, and from the inhabitants of China, but use, with these last people, the same written characters; a proof that the Chinese characters are like hieroglyphics, independent of language."—*Jamieson's Rhet.*, p. 18. "The Japanese, the Tonquinese, and the Corceans, who speak different languages from one another, and from the inhabitants of China, use, however, the same written characters with them; and by this means correspond intelligibly with each other in writing, though ignorant of the language spoken in their several countries; a plain proof," &c.—*Blair's Rhet.*, p. 67. "The curved line is made square instead of round, for the reason beforementioned."—*Knight, on the Greek Alphabet*, p. 6. "Every one should content himself with the use of those tones only that he is habituated to in speech, and to give none other to emphasis, but what he would do to the same words in discourse. Thus whatever he utters will be done with ease, and appear natural."—*Sheridan's Elocution*, p. 103. "Stops, or pauses, are a total cessation of sound during a perceptible, and in numerous compositions, a measurable space of time."—*Ib.*, p. 104. "Pauses or rests, in speaking and reading, are a total cessation of the voice during a perceptible, and, in many cases, a measurable space of time."—*Murray's Gram.*, p. 248; *English Reader*, p. 13; *Goldsbury's Gr.*, 76; *Kirkham's*, 208; *Felton's*, 133; *et al.* "Nouns which express a small one of the kind are called *Diminutive Nouns*; as, lambkin, hillock, satchel, gosling, from lamb, hill, sack, goose."—*Bullions, E. Gram.*, 1837, p. 9. "What is the cause that nonsense so often escapes being detected, both by the writer and by the reader?"—*Campbell's Rhet.*, p. xi, and 280. "An Interjection is a word used to express sudden emotion. They are so called, because they are generally thrown in between the parts of a sentence without reference to the structure of the other parts of it."—*M'Culloch's Gram.*, p. 36. "*Ought* (in duty bound) *oughtest, oughtedst*, are it's only inflections."—*Mackintosh's Gram.*, p. 165. "But the arrangment, government, agreement, and dependence of one word upon another, are referred to our reason."—*Osborn's Key, Pref.*, p. 3. "*Me* is a personal pronoun, first person singular, and the accusative case."—*Guy's Gram.*, p. 20. "The substantive *self* is added to a pronoun; as, herself, himself, &c.; and when thus united, is called a reciprocal pronoun."—*Ib.*, p. 18. "One cannot avoid thinking that our author had done better to have begun the first of these three sentences, with saying, *it is novelty which bestows charms on a monster*, &c."—*Blair's Rhet.*, p. 207. "The idea which they present to us of nature's resembling art, of art's being considered as an original, and nature as a copy,[451] seems not very distinct nor well brought out, nor indeed very material to our author's purpose."—*Ib.*, p. 220. "The present construction of the sentence, has plainly been owing to hasty and careless writing."—*Ib.*, p. 220. "Adverbs serve to modify, or to denote some circumstance of an action, or of a quality, relative to its time, place, order, degree, and the other properties of it, which we have occasion to specify."—*Ib.*, p. 84. "The more that any nation is improved by science, and the more perfect their language becomes, we may naturally expect that it will abound more with connective particles."—*Ib.*, p. 85. "Mr. Greenleaf's book is by far the best adapted for learners of any that has yet appeared on the subject."—DR. FELTUS and BP. ONDERDONK: *Greenleaf's Gram.*, p. 2. "Punctuation is the art of marking in writing the several pauses, or rests, between sentences, and the parts of sentences, according to their proper quantity or proportion, as they are expressed in a just and accurate pronunciation."—*Lowth's Gram.*, p. 114. "A compound sentence must be resolved into simple ones, and separated by commas."—*Greenleaf's Gram.*, p. 41; *Allen Fisk's*, 155.[452] "Simple sentences should be separated from each other by commas, unless such sentences are connected by a conjunction: as, 'Youth is passing away, age is approaching and death is near.'"—*Hall's Gram.*, p. 36. "*V* has the sound of flat *f*, and bears the same relation to it, as *b* does to *p*, *d* to *t*, hard *g* to *k*, and *z* to *s*. It has one uniform sound."—*Murray's Gram.*, p. 17; *Fisk's*, 42. "*V* is flat *f*, and bears the same relation to it as *b* does to *p*, *d* to *t*, hard *g* to *k*, and *z* to *s*. It is never irregular."—*Walker's Dict.*, p. 52. "*V* has the sound of flat *f*; and bears the same relation to it as *z* does to *s*. It has one uniform sound."—*Greenleaf's Gram.*, p. 20. "The author is explaining the distinction, between the powers of sense and imagination in the human mind."—*Murray's Gram.*, 8vo, Vol. i, p. 343. [The author is endeavouring] "to explain a very abstract point, the distinction between the powers of sense and imagination in the human mind."—*Blair's Rhet.*, p. 164. "HE (Anglo-Saxon *he*) is a Personal pronoun, of the Third Person, Masculine Gender (Decline he), of the singular number, in the nominative case."—*Fowler's E. Gram.*, 8vo, 1850, §589.

FALSE SYNTAX UNDER THE CRITICAL NOTES.

UNDER CRITICAL NOTE I.—OF THE PARTS OF SPEECH.

"The passive voice denotes a being acted upon."—*Maunders Gram.*, p. 6.

[FORMULE.—Not proper, because the term "*being acted upon*" as here used, suggests a doubt concerning its classification in parsing. But, according to Critical Note 1st, "Words that may constitute different parts of speech, must not be left doubtful as to their classification, or to what part of speech they belong." Therefore, the phraseology should be altered; thus, "The passive voice denotes *an action received*." Or; "The passive voice denotes *the receiving of an* action."]

"Milton, in some of his prose works, has very finely turned periods."—*Blair's Rhet.*, p. 127; *Jamieson's*, 129. "These will be found to be all, or chiefly, of that class."—*Blair's Rhet.*, p. 32. "All appearances of an author's affecting harmony, are disagreeable."—*Ib.*, p. 127; *Jamieson*, 128. "Some nouns have a double increase, that is, increase by more syllables than one; as, *iter, itin~eris*."—*Adam's Gram.*, p. 255; *Gould's*, 241. "The powers of man are enlarged by advancing cultivation."—*Gurney's Essays*, p. 62. "It is always important to begin well; to make a favourable impression at first setting out."—*Blair's Rhet.*, p. 307. "For if one take a wrong method at first setting out, it will lead him astray in all that follows."—*Ib.*, 313. "His mind is full of his subject, and his words are all expressive."—*Ib.*, 179. "How exquisitely is this all performed in Greek!"—*Harris's Hermes*, p. 422. "How little is all this to satisfy the ambition of an immortal soul!"—

Murray's Key, 8vo, p. 253. "So as to exhibit the object in its full and most striking point of view."—*Blair's Rhet.*, p. 41. "And that the author know how to descend with propriety to the plain, as well as how to rise to the bold and figured style."—*Ib.*, p. 401. "The heart can only answer to the heart."—*Ib.*, p. 259. "Upon its first being perceived."—*Harris's Hermes*, p. 229. "Call for Samson, that he may make us sport."—*Judges*, xvi, 25. "And he made them sport."—*Ibid.* "The term *suffer* in this definition is used in a technical sense, and means simply the receiving of an action, or the being acted upon."—*Bullions*, p. 29. "The Text is what is only meant to be taught in Schools."—*Brightland, Pref.*, p. ix. "The perfect participle denotes action or being perfected or finished."— *Kirkham's Gram.*, p. 78. "From the intricacy and confusion which are produced by their being blended together."—*Murray's Gram.*, 8vo, p. 66. "This very circumstance of a word's being employed antithetically, renders it important in the sentence."—*Kirkham's Elocution*, p. 121. "It [the pronoun *that*] is applied to both persons and things."—*Murray's Gram.*, p. 53. "Concerning us, as being every where evil spoken of."—*Barclay's Works*, Vol. ii, p. vi. "Every thing beside was buried in a profound silence."—*Steele.* "They raise more full conviction than any reasonings produce."—*Blair's Rhet.*, p. 367. "It appears to me no more than a fanciful refinement."—*Ib.*, p. 436. "The regular resolution throughout of a complete passage."—*Churchill's Gram.*, p. vii. "The infinitive is known by its being immediately preceded by the word *to*."—*Maunders Gram.*, p. 6. "It will not be gaining much ground to urge that the basket, or vase, is understood to be the capital."—*Kames, El. of Crit.*, Vol. ii, p. 356. "The disgust one has to drink ink in reality, is not to the purpose where the subject is drinking ink figuratively."—*Ib.*, ii, 231. "That we run not into the extreme of pruning so very close."—*Blair's Rhet.*, p. 111. "Being obliged to rest for a little on the preposition by itself."—*Ib.*, p. 112; *Jamieson's Rhet.*, 93. "Being obliged to rest a little on the preposition by itself."—*Murray's Gram.*, p. 319. "Our days on the earth are as a shadow, and there is none abiding."—*1 Chron.*, xxix, 15. "There maybe a more particular expression attempted, of certain objects, by means of resembling sounds."—*Blair's Rhet.*, p. 129; *Jamieson's*, 130; *Murray's Gram.*, 331. "The right disposition of the shade, makes the light and colouring strike the more."—*Blair's Rhet.*, 144. "I observed that a diffuse style inclines most to long periods."—*Ib.*, p. 178. "Their poor Arguments, which they only Pickt up and down the Highway "—*Divine Right of Tythes*, p. iii. "Which must be little, but a transcribing out of their writings."—*Barclay's Works*, iii, 353. "That single impulse is a forcing out of almost all the breath."—*Rush, on the Voice*, p. 254. "Picini compares modulation to the turning off from a road."—*Gardiner's Music of Nature*, p. 405. "So much has been written, on and off, of almost every subject."—*The Friend*, ii, 117. "By reading books written by the best authors, his mind became highly improved."—*Murray's Key*, 8vo, p. 201. "For I never made the being richly provided a token of a spiritual ministry."—*Barclay's Works*, iii, 470.

UNDER CRITICAL NOTE II.—OF DOUBTFUL REFERENCE.

"However disagreeable, we must resolutely perform our duty."—*Murray's Key*, 8vo, p. 171.

[FORMULE.—Not proper, because the adjective *disagreeable* appears to relate to the pronoun *we*, though such a relation was probably not intended by the author. But, according to Critical Note 2d, "The reference of words to other words, or their syntactical relation according to the sense, should never be left doubtful, by any one who means to be understood." The sentence may be amended thus: "However disagreeable *the task*, we must resolutely perform our duty."]

"The formation of verbs in English, both regular and irregular, is derived from the Saxon."—*Lowth's Gram.*, p. 47. "Time and chance have an influence on all things human, and on nothing more remarkably than on language."—*Campbell's Rhet.*, p. 180. "Time and chance have an influence on all things human, and on nothing more remarkable than on language."—*Jamieson's Rhet.*, p. 47. "Archytases being a virtuous man, who happened to perish once upon a time, is with him a sufficient ground," &c.—*Philological Museum*, i, 466. "He will be the better qualified to understand, with accuracy, the meaning of a numerous class of words, in which they form a material part."—*Murray's Gram.*, 8vo, p. 120. "We should continually have the goal in view, which would direct us in the race."—*Murray's Key*, 8vo, p. 172. "But [Addison's figures] seem to rise of their own accord from the subject, and constantly embellish it."—*Blair's Rhet.*, p. 150; *Jamieson's*, 157. "As far as persons and other animals and things that we can see go, it is very easy to distinguish Nouns."—*Cobbett's Gram.*, ¶14. "Dissyllables ending in *y, e* mute, or accented on the last syllable, may be sometimes compared like monosyllables."—*Frost's El. of Gram.*, p. 12. "Admitting the above objection, it will not overrule the design."—*Rush, on the Voice*, p. 140. "These philosophical innovators forget, that objects are like men, known only by their actions."—*Dr. Murray's Hist. of Lang.*, i, 326. "The connexion between words and ideas is arbitrary and conventional, owing to the agreement of men among themselves."—*Jamieson's Rhet.*, p. 1. "The connexion between words and ideas may, in general, be considered as arbitrary and conventional, owing to the agreement of men among themselves."—*Blair's Rhet.*, p. 53. "A man whose inclinations led him to be corrupt, and had great abilities to manage and multiply and defend his corruptions."—*Swift*. "They have no more control over him than any other men."—*Wayland's Moral Science*, 1st Ed., p. 372. "His old words are all true English, and numbers exquisite."—*Spectator*, No. 540. "It has been said, that not only Jesuits can equivocate."—*Murray's Exercises*, 8vo, p. 121. "It has been said, that Jesuits can not only equivocate."—*Murray's Key*, 8vo, p. 253. "The nominative of the first and second person in Latin is seldom expressed."—*Adam's Gram.*, p. 154; *Gould's*, 157. "Some words are the same in both numbers."—*Murray's Gram.*, 8vo, p. 40; *Ingersoll's*, 18; *Fisk's*, 59; *Kirkham's*, 39; *W. Allen's*, 42; et al. "Some nouns are the same in both numbers."—*Merchant's Gram.*, p. 29; *Smith's*, 45; et al. "Others are the same in both numbers; as, *deer, swine, &c.*"—*Frost's El. of Gram.*, p. 8. "The following list denotes the sounds of the consonants, being in number twenty-two."—*Murray's Gram.*, p. 6; *Fisk's*, 36. "And is the ignorance of these peasants a reason for others to remain ignorant; or to render the subject a less becoming inquiry?"—*Harris's Hermes*, p. 293; *Murray's Gram.*, 8vo, p. 288. "He is one of the most correct, and perhaps the best, of our prose writers."—*Lowth's Gram., Pref.*, p. iv., "The motions of a vortex and a whirlwind are perfectly similar."—*Jamieson's Rhet.*, p. 131. "What I have been saying throws light upon one important verse in the Bible, which I should like to have read."—*Abbott's Teacher*, p. 182. "When there are any circumstances of time, place, or other limitations, which the principal object of our sentence requires to have connected with it."—*Blair's Rhet.*, p. 115; *Jamieson's Rhet.*, 98; *Murray's Gram.*, i, 322. "Interjections are words used to express emotion, affection, or passion, and imply suddenness."—*Bucke's Gram.*, p. 77. "But the genitive is only used to express the measure of things in the plural number."—*Adam's Gram.*, p. 200; *Gould's*, 198. "The buildings of the institution have been enlarged; the expense of which, added to the increased price of provisions, renders it necessary to advance the terms of admission."—*Murray's Key*, 8vo, p. 183. "These sentences are far less difficult than complex."—*S. S. Greene's Analysis, or Grammar*, 1st Ed., p. 179.

END

Milton Keynes UK
Ingram Content Group UK Ltd.
UKHW050137080424
440718UK00003B/34